IHATOR BROWN

START WITH A BUSINESS PLAN

A Step-by-Step Guide to Write a Simple and Successful Business Plan

First edition

This book was professionally typeset on Reedsy.
Find out more at reedsy.com

Contents

1

Chapter 1 - Introduction

Are you aware that 90% of new enterprises fail? Seventy-five per cent of businesses that are successful in securing venture capital, a testament to their creative product ideas, fail within the first five years of operation. You need more than just a good product proposition to establish a new business. To be one of the 10% of entrepreneurs that thrive, you must have a clearly defined vision and consistently implement it. To put it another way, a well-established corporate plan is required. The most common reasons for a company's inception failing include, among other things, a lack of focus, a lack of domain-specific business experience required for the company to thrive in today's highly competitive environment, and a lack of a solid business strategy. As the data above shows, rushing into investing money without addressing these fundamentals does not guarantee success.

According to Forbes, every company idea, if properly fostered before implementation, has the potential to join the 10% and grow into a multi-million-dollar corporation. Are you thinking of starting your own business? The first step toward success is to focus on defining and expressing your vision via developing a corporate strategy. Consequently, you will rediscover and intensify your passion for the objective, providing you with the drive to see the vision through to completion. But where do you start? Is it feasible to write a business plan on your own, or do you need the assistance of a consultant? A business strategy is made up of many distinct parts. How do you develop and present a corporate plan that everyone understands? What methods do you employ?

This book is a step-by-step guide to help you answer all of the above questions. Consequently, you will gain the confidence to develop a robust and well-structured business plan. In addition, this book will address all of the problems highlighted above and help you understand the importance and benefits of establishing a business plan in general. This book can help you understand, develop, and write your business plan.

2

Chapter 2: Fundamentals of a Business Plan

B usiness plans are written statements that describe and assess your company's activities and provide detailed projections regarding the business's future operations and financial position. It also tackles the financial aspects of starting or establishing a business, such as how much money you'll need, what you'll do with the money once you've created your company and the business plan's other aspects. Writing a business strategy requires a great amount of effort is required. So, what's the purpose of devoting the necessary time to creating one? The most valuable response comes from the collective wisdom of literally millions of other business owners who have gone before you in their endeavours. It has been shown that the majority of business owners who have written plans are content with them, whereas the majority of business owners who do not have written plans regret not having done so.

2.1 Why develop a business plan?

The more specific and immediate benefits of creating your business plan are discussed below.

The vast majority of lenders and investors will not consider your concept seriously until you have a written business plan in your possession. Some landlords will not lease space to you unless you have a sound business plan before you begin looking for a premise. Before committing to you, they want to see that you have completely analyzed the significant obstacles you will encounter as a business owner and have a solid grasp of your sector before committing to you. Aside from that, they want to ensure that your company has a high likelihood of long-term success. Approximately 35% to 40% of those actively engaged in business are unaware of how money flows through their company.

Writing a business plan with the assistance of this book will educate you on where the money comes from and where it goes when it is earned. If you ask your financial supporters to go through your approach before considering awarding you the cash you need, it shouldn't surprise you. It is estimated that there are two times more prospective lenders and investors than possible company owners. As long as you have a well-thought-out business and financial plan that has a good chance of success and you are persistent, you will be able to get the cash you want. Of course, it may take longer and require more work than you imagine, but if you have faith in your company, you will succeed.

One of the book's major themes could come as a surprise to you at first glance. It's as simple as it is crucial in this situation. Before anybody else will consider your proposal, you must be persuaded of its legitimacy as the prospective business owner. Consequently, most of the jobs you need to do here have a dual purpose in the natural world. Its goal is to provide thorough answers to all prospective lender's and investors' questions about the financial services industry. It will also reveal how money moves through your business, its strengths and weaknesses, and your true chances of success.

When it comes to operating a small business, there are no certainties, but nothing is more certain than the lengthy planning process explained in this book. But it should help you detect and rectify faults in your business model, which you should be able to deal with it. If the findings of this study suggest that your idea will not be successful, it may be feasible to forego the start-up or expansion of your business. It is quite important to comprehend this. Some businesses have been successful because they didn't start a company with problems at the start. This should come as no surprise to anyone who has been in business.

Writing a strategy helps you realize how changing certain components of your business plan could increase sales or assist you in achieving other goals you have set for yourself. There is no need to invest any money to experiment with various parts of your company's operations. Using a computer spreadsheet to generate financial projections makes it much simpler to compare and contrast different alternatives since it enables you to do so much more quickly. Your chances of achieving success are boosted due to your ability to fine-tune your tactics and business design. Pretend you're in the following situation: You have a business plan to start a company that would import Korean leather jackets into the United States of America. Everything seems to be in working order during the first run-through of your strategy.

As a result of your investigation into exchange rate fluctuations, you have concluded that boosting your profit margin on the jackets will be required to compensate for anticipated future declines in dollar purchasing power. That your price remains comparable with that of other coats and that your average profits will increase as a consequence of this alteration is shown to you. There is also a good chance that exchange rates could go down soon, so you are now protected.

A business may be seen as a game of chance, one way of looking at it. Your money and the money of a bank or an investor are placed at risk when you start or establish a company from scratch. Assuming your predictions are true, you will make a profit and be able to pay back the debts, which will delight everyone. If, on the other hand, your estimate proves to be erroneous, both you and the bank or investors may suffer money losses and the emotional distress that comes with failing. Naturally, the bank is safe because it owns the collateral used to get the loan.

Important things to consider are: what is a business plan, and what is the objective of having a company strategy in the first place? The benefits of a business plan can only be fully appreciated after the reasons for their creation and the steps involved in their development are well understood.

In its most basic form, an organisation's business plan describes the business in considerable detail, including its goals and the tactics it intends to pursue those goals and objectives. Business plans are often prepared for start-up firms, but they may also be written for existing businesses. Business plans are written for a variety of reasons. The plan addresses, among other things, the venture's operational, financial, and marketing components.

The development of a business plan is vital for every startup since it gives direction for the company's future growth. For starters, it is essential since a business plan is one of the major requirements for venture capital organizations and banks interested in investing funds in small and medium-sized businesses. For this reason, it is essential. The executive summary is followed by a full explanation of the company, including its goods and services, and a section explaining how the business expects to accomplish its goals from the viewpoints of operations, finance, and marketing, among other things. Also, the business plan is a quick look at the industry the company will be in and a description of how the company plans to stand out from its competitors.

2.2 The different types of plans

There are many different types of business strategies to take into consideration. Feasibility studies, annual plans, internal plans, operations plans, and growth plans are examples of what is included in this category of planning. These many types of plans are developed to meet the particular requirements of various business situations. For example, suppose you are preparing a business plan for internal reasons rather than seeking financing from a financial institution. In that case, it is not required to provide background information in your business plan. While creating a business plan for external investors, it is vital to include information about the management team. However, when writing a business plan for a bank, it is not required to provide information about the company's financial history and past. Depending on the circumstances of the issue at hand, several pieces of information are included in the business plan to help the company succeed.

2.3 Business plans for small and medium-sized

When it comes to outlining all of the actions that a new company must take to achieve its goals, the business plan you prepare for a startup is as straightforward as it gets in detail. A typical business plan includes information on the company's financial analysis, implementation milestones, the management team and the business's overall strategy, and several projections about the marketplace and the company's product or service offering.

Estimates for the company's sales, profit, loss, cash flow, and balance sheet are included in the plan, as are expectations for the company's financial performance. In addition to the monthly estimates for the first year of the project, it is anticipated that the section on financial analysis will contain additional financial analysis tables. The business plan for a startup often consists of an abstract and an appendix at the end of the document.

2.4 Internal business plans

An internal business plan is a business plan that is not intended for submission to a financial institution, an external investor, or any other third party for review. In such plans, there is no practical need to go into considerable detail about the company or the management team that is being discussed. In addition, you can decide whether or not to include financial estimations such as forecasts and a budget in your proposal or proposal package. A typical internal business plan is written in the style of a report, with each paragraph representing a different element of the overall plan. According to the format chosen, the key points of a PowerPoint presentation will be displayed as bullet points or as slides, respectively.

2.5 Business operational plan

Operational business plans are often developed just for internal use, constituting a kind of internal business plan in the strictest meaning of the phrase. Besides that, these papers, called annual plans, give specific information about deadlines, implementation milestones, specific dates, and the roles of teams and their supervisors.

The operational business plan does not detail who is accountable for what and when it is to be accomplished, but it does provide a general overview. Duty and deadlines are analyzed from top priority and high-level priority standpoints, and the results are presented in a table. The majority of the time, it is used to arrange content in the form of bullet points on slides in a presenting environment. There is no need for this paper to describe the management teams or the business. Another disadvantage of this company's plans is that there are no in-depth explanations of any financial projections. When it comes to formulating plans, they are often not considered when a company's overall strategy is formed and implemented.

2.6 Expansion strategies

It is possible that some company plans aren't concerned with how the business will operate in its entirety. Instead, they are entirely interested in a certain business sector or a specific element of the company's activities. They are referred to by many names, depending on what they intend to achieve, such as growth plans, new product plans, and expansion plans. Internal plans may or may not be considered, depending on whether they are meant to attract outside investment or meet a financial institution's lending conditions. For example, suppose your company is just getting started, and you want to put up a startup plan to seek more funding from investors. Develop a growth plan if you need to acquire more funds or get any kind of loan financing for your company.

A complete description of the business and important background information on each management team member should be included in both plans. A growth plan meant for internal consumption by the company, on the other hand, will be categorized as an internal business plan and will not contain information about the business or management team. The need to consider the company's steps to expand and grow internally while developing internal expansion and development plans cannot be overstated. Internal money, which the company in question provides, is included in such internal plans. It is conceivable that detailed financial projections will be published or that they will not. However, when it comes to expansion plans, the estimates of sales and costs are often given in great detail.

2.7 The benefits of a strategic plan

It may be advantageous to write a business plan for several reasons, some of which are listed below. This part will discuss some of the benefits of building a business plan for your company and some of the potential drawbacks this process may have for your business. Most of the time, a company will only write a business plan if they seek money or investment for their business or enterprise in question. Often, people don't like it because it can be hard and take a long time to finish.

Since business planning is, in essence, a technique of distancing the business owner from the day-to-day operations of their company and enabling them to think about the big picture from time to time, it may be a highly successful practice. Every business owner understands that spending more time working in the business than on the business takes up a disproportionate amount of their time. A business plan may free up the time of shareholders or directors, allowing them to focus on the company's strategy, projections, and predictions and establish a broad sense of direction for the company. When done right, this is quite effective. It has been repeatedly shown that a company with a clearly defined goal and direction is far more likely to be successful than a corporation just responding to the business that it receives.

When putting out a business plan, it is common for people to be encouraged to think outside the box, particularly when considering issues such as Porter's 5 forces. As a result, people and businesses will be better able to look at things that could have a big impact on the growth and development of their businesses.

In addition to the several different business plan templates that are easily available, business plan examples can be utilized to streamline the process and make it a lot less complicated. Using this format, you will be able to guarantee that your business plan has coverage for all of the important parts.

Lenders and equity investors, for the most part, will require a business plan to be submitted as part of their application process; in fact, this is frequently the reason why businesses create a business plan in the first place. If you follow a well-structured approach, you will be able to present a very professional image of your company to possible lenders or investors. Suppose you are willing to devote the required time and effort to developing your business plan. In that case, you will most likely obtain a prompter answer from a financial credit institution or an investor. On the other hand, if you do not devote the essential time and effort to developing your business plan, you will almost certainly obtain a delayed response from a financial institution or investor.

2.7.1 The clarity of the plan

A business plan may assist in explaining the decision-making process when it comes to critical elements of a company's operations, such as capital investments, leasing, personnel, and other similar matters. Of course, you will not be able to complete all of your tasks. However, a well-written business plan will aid you in defining the most important objectives and milestones for your company on which you should focus your efforts.

2.8 Creating a marketing strategy

Market research is a key component of every company's overall business plan. This analysis process assists in identifying your target market(s), target consumers, and the method by which you will promote and position your product/service concerning these markets and customers.

2.9 Assistance with financial resources

For many businesses, whether they are searching for bank loans or capital from investors, a business plan that tackles issues of profitability and income development is required at some point.

2.10 The retention of top-tier talent

The ability of a company to grow to attract excellent personnel and business partners is crucial. A business strategy is created to aid in recruiting competent people at the proper time. Employees want to know what the company's vision is, how it plans to achieve its goals, and how they can make a difference in their employment due to that vision being realized.

2.10.1 It creates a foundation for discussion

Structural support is provided by a company plan, which also clearly states the objectives of corporate administration. It serves as a reference tool, assisting the business in staying on track with sales objectives and operational milestones. When used correctly and with regular help, it may help you keep an eye on and control your main focus areas.

2.11 Writing a business plan

Successful companies are built on well-thought-out and meticulously produced business and strategic plans. Essentially, it specifies the goals and objectives of the business and the strategies and tactics that will be used to attain those goals. A business marketing and financial strategy should be included in this document. It should also contain detailed information on where the company is heading and how it wants to get there. It is possible to significantly simplify starting a new company by creating a business plan before launching. Business plans are akin to road maps for a company's operations in that they outline how the company will operate. It defines objectives and assigns a priority to certain operations.

- A comprehensive business plan may also be necessary when applying for a loan to start a business or for investment capital to expand an existing business. Most lenders want a business plan before considering lending money to a certain business. Based on the information included in the plan, the lender will be able to judge whether or not the business has a good chance of succeeding. According to the American Bankers Association, lenders are more likely to provide a loan to a company with a well-thought-out business plan because it appears to be a less risky investment than a company with an incomplete or sloppy strategy because it appears to be a less risky investment.

- If you want to be successful in business, your company plan should have the following elements:
- After reading the executive summary, the lender should be persuaded that the company is worth their time and money. It should contain a high-level overview of the plan, including services or items, workers, necessary money, and how it will be used. If the executive summary isn't succinct, full of energy, and excited about the company, the rest of the plan may be skipped entirely.
- The table of contents gives a high-level overview of each part of the plan and the appendices that come with it.
- If the company already exists, a company description will be provided. This part should contain any important facts or achievements and prior earnings and financial information that you would want to highlight. It should be done in a forward-looking manner to draw it to a close, with new projects being prepared for the future.
- It should be encouraged for people to explain their product or service in simple English. There should be no jargon or acronyms since they may generate misunderstandings among venture capitalists or other possible investors in the company. They understand how money works, but they may not know the exact product or service.
- Exceptional results should be achieved with this component of the marketing strategy. It should include market analysis and information on distribution techniques and relevant regulations, among other things. It should make available any marketing information readily available to the public.

- When it comes to loans, this is especially important since it proves to lenders that the individuals requesting the loan are acquainted with the market in which they want to invest. They may trust this company by putting their money into it. An effective plan for maximizing the market's potential must also be included. The strategy should include a vast amount of information and many different approaches.
- The financial section should contain statistics and be completed by a trained specialist in finance. If appropriate for the document, graphs and flow charts may be placed in the appendices. In addition, a minimum cost projection for the next year, which should include start-up expenses and a profit and loss analysis and predicted sales numbers for the following year, should be included if the company is new.
- The management section includes images of the members of the executive team. Because lenders are more inclined to grant money to a group of managers who have developed a successful company from the bottom up, any degrees gained or other business successes should be stated in the application. In addition, when a company's strategy is being developed, a person with exceptional credentials may be nominated as an advisor or even be appointed to the board of directors.

2.12 Developing a company strategy

A company's inception and growth into a successful corporation is a time-consuming and challenging process that requires dedication and perseverance. It is nearly impossible to establish a company and see it grow into a lucrative operation without first developing a good business strategy. Developing a business strategy is one of the most important activities that every entrepreneur can do. This method provides immeasurable benefits to the company's development and is very beneficial to managing a successful commercial enterprise. Having a well-written, carefully thought-out business plan is proof of concept, financial justification, and a road map to success for a company or business.

An idea is the starting point for the vast majority of aspiring entrepreneurs, who then use their initiative and some kind of financing to produce a service or product based on that notion. Developing a business plan facilitates an entrepreneur's ability to thoroughly flesh out all of the benefits and drawbacks, possibilities and dangers involved with their idea.

To determine whether or not a business plan has the potential to be successful, entrepreneurs must devote the required time and resources to studying and analyzing all of the relevant aspects of the market. It is intended to act as a proof of concept. The vast majority of the time, this technique results in adjustments to the original idea that will help it overcome the obstacles that have been revealed as a result of the process itself.

The preparation of financial projections is a critically important component of developing a company plan. All that is necessary to make financial projections is an estimate of the potential company owner's financial resources required to launch their concept and an estimation of the financial consequences that the concept will generate. Entrepreneurs should consider these elements when developing their business strategies to determine how much money they will need to invest in themselves or raise from others and what type of return they can reasonably expect on their investment in the future.

Because entrepreneurs are, by nature, optimistic people, the ability to be realistic when making financial estimates is one of the most important and difficult components of producing financial estimates for them. Genuine and realistic financial projections assist in the financial justification of a business strategy, not only for the entrepreneur but also for potential outside investors who may be interested in the endeavour on which the projections are made.

A business plan and financial projections are created, and the plan is then put into action. The plan acts as a road map for the company's founder to follow. As a road map directs a traveller through a variety of options while travelling a route, the concepts, ideas, and statistics included in a business plan may influence the entrepreneur's decisions on a variety of issues, including financing, employee recruitment and acquisition, and equipment acquisition, among others. In contrast to a road map, which remains stationary, a well-written strategy is a dynamic document that changes in reaction to new information or changing circumstances. Although things may change, the business plan's basic ideas, especially the financial projections, help make sense of the next steps.

Successful entrepreneurs will begin with a basic notion and transform it into a large and long-lasting commercial business through devotion, tenacity, and luck. In starting a company, one of the most important things an entrepreneur can do is create a business plan that outlines their goals and objectives. It will be quite useful to any company owner to have a well-thought-out business plan, and it will be vital to the success of the venture.

3

Chapter 3: Assessing the Business Concept

E very year, around one million new businesses are established in the United States, ranging from small home-based enterprises to large multinational corporations, many of which require hundreds of millions of dollars in start-up capital. According to predictions, just one in every five of these new businesses will make it to their fifth anniversary and achieve the objectives they promised when they first started. That is an alarming figure! What might be the source of this occurrence if just one out of every five enterprises in the "Land of Opportunity" survives even for a relatively short period? While there are many reasons for this, the most common one is also the most treatable. There is no magic recipe for success, but one essential rule applies: "A company owner or management that fails to plan must plan to fail." Business plans help entrepreneurs and managers develop strategies, balance their enthusiasm with reality, and recognize their limitations.

Undercapitalization, negative cash flow, hiring the wrong people, selecting the wrong location, underestimating your competition, and pursuing a market in the wrong industry are all examples of potentially disastrous blunders. It takes time to build an effective corporate strategy. Plan to spend 50 to 150 hours creating a full and detailed business plan that includes research, documentation, analysis, and review. Entrepreneurs should start preparing at least six months before they hope to develop, expand, or obtain finance for their company. Most entrepreneurs will need to devote time to their start-up while either working another job or, if they are expanding an existing business, they will need to handle the day-to-day operations of the company they are expanding. Six months allows you to refine and focus on your company's ideas and concepts while also analyzing your assumptions and hypotheses.

3.1 Starting the voyage

There are various choices for each of us to create our own business and earn a livelihood. Several possibilities range from thousands of home-based businesses to various small, medium, and large-sized businesses in the manufacturing, distribution, retail, and service sectors. According to estimates, the top 20 enterprises in the United States employ just around 20% of the country's workforce. It comprises personnel from local, state, and federal governments and nonprofit organizations and entrepreneurs like yourself, who are willing to enter the market and take considerable risks to chart their route and live life on their terms.

Written business plans may help you get your journey started off on the right foot and avoid pitfalls that entrepreneurs get into when shooting from the hip and relying on inaccurate, incomplete, or incorrect assumptions. Several individuals contact lenders and investors with ideas, concepts, and technology that they felt would be certain hits throughout the years. As part of the business planning process, they conducted extensive research into what they wanted to do. Unfortunately, they discovered that their "surefire winner" was nothing more than a pipe dream for various reasons, including undercapitalization, incorrect market timing, insufficient market size, poor management or people skills, or poor products or services. Before you start this journey, you should think about many things. These things will help you figure out whether or not what you're planning is good for you and the market.

Before you start a new business, think about how it might affect you, your family, and your other relationships:

- As a consequence, your profits will be reduced.
- Your working hours will expand at a rapid pace.
- Relationships with your family will be strained.
- You'll either spend all of your money or get into debt.
- You will sometimes feel as though you are going behind schedule.
- It's conceivable that you'll become more irritable or judgmental towards others.
- Consequently, you'll spend less time with your friends and family.
- You may get more headaches, backaches, or stomachaches.
- If you are not working, you will have emotions of guilt on occasion.
- It may seem like your life is fully devoted to work for a while.

Second, ask yourself the following questions:

- How much money do I need to invest in this business?
- Is it feasible for me to get more investors?
- What type of return am I hoping to get?
- What precisely do I excel at?
- What do I like doing the most, and what brings me the most pleasure when I do it?
- Will I be willing to put in more effort and work for a longer period?
- What can I do to make amends for my errors?
- Will I make time for my development regularly?

3.2 What is required of you

If you are currently employed, you have firsthand knowledge of what it is like to be a part of the labour force. If you think that starting your own company entails doing the same things as everyone else, you're in for a nice surprise. If you are creating a business plan to start a small business, you should be aware that small-business owners are responsible for the whole operation, which involves much more than simply providing goods or services. When you start your own business, you will most likely be responsible for all of the administrative and managerial obligations that your present company currently does.

To determine your fit for business ownership, you must first grasp the responsibilities that come with the job. This section discusses what it takes to manage a business and your responsibilities as a business owner. If you've always wanted to start your own business but have never done it before, this is a great place to start. Consider the following issue: What exactly goes into running a successful business? Do you have the skills required to finish the task? Every company has a stressed-out executive who complains about being overworked because he must simultaneously wear two or three hats. Everyone has heard the tale. Small business owners would do anything to have to wear two or three hats for the rest of their lives!

Sales taxes and payroll or self-employment taxes must be collected, and the associated documentation and payments. Accounts receivable must be collected as soon as possible, funds must be deposited in a bank account, and account payable must be paid. Providing outstanding customer service, having the appropriate equipment and supplies on hand, monitoring and controlling inventories, and tracking and keeping work in progress are critical roles in most businesses. This is in addition to the things you'll have to do for your customers, which will take up most of your time.

As a business owner, you may expect to be responsible for several tasks, some of which are as follows:

- There will undoubtedly be moments when you feel the need to change things, whether developing the company or offering a new product line. If you wish to make a difference, it will be your responsibility to see that change through. You will need to plan it out and put it into action, and you will need to consider all of the consequences of your decision before making it.
- To build or grow your business, you must first determine who your customers are and where they are located. This is something that market researchers can assist you with. As a business owner, you may be required to do market research at various points over the life of your company, such as when considering the launch of a new product.
- Sales, marketing, and advertising executives: You will not only be in charge of creating your marketing or advertising strategy but also of putting it into action. You might be in charge of drafting advertising copy, doing preliminary market research, visiting potential clients, and ensuring that existing customers are happy. Depending on your business, you may be forced to join business groups, attend multiple breakfasts, lunches, and dinners, and generally network with everyone who might help your company grow and thrive.
- Accountant: Even if you have an accountant, you will need to understand accounting fundamentals such as which records to keep and how to organize them appropriately. If you do not have an accountant, you will be responsible for filing all tax forms and learning how to prepare and evaluate all financial accounts.
- If you sell items at retail and are responsible for collecting sales tax on behalf of various government organizations, you are a tax collector. If you have employees, you are responsible for collecting payroll taxes from them and punctually filing monthly and quarterly tax forms with the relevant government agency.
- A bill collector is someone who goes about collecting money from consumers. You must collect money from customers who do not pay

their bills. To recover the funds you owe, you must first understand what you can and cannot do. You must also decide on the most efficient manner of collecting money and when to give up.

- If you have employees, you will be in charge of all human resource-related activities, such as recruiting, hiring, firing, and keeping track of all employee benefits information. Along with this duty comes the need to complete all insurance documentation, reply to employee enquiries and complaints, and decide whether or not to change the benefits package you give to your employees.

- Lawyer: Even if you have a lawyer, you must be familiar with the legal system. You will have to do many things if you don't hire an attorney. For example, you'll have to write all of your contracts and other legal documents, and you'll also have to know about any employment rules that apply whether you have employees or are hiring.

- You will almost definitely depend on your computer as a business owner, and you will be expected to load software, apply updates, and fix the computer when it fails. You'll also need to keep up with new products and technological advances as they become available.

- Clerk/Receptionist/Typist/Secretary: Even if you have clerical support, you will have to do some filing, typing, mailing, and answering the phone. Because you'll need to be knowledgeable about various tasks, you'll need to be able to teach people what to do when you've hired help. It is critical that you thoroughly examine this list of the most important activities required in running a business to begin to estimate your chances of success realistically. You will be spending a large amount of time dealing with the responsibilities that have been put on you as a business owner. If you want to be successful, you must complete your task within the time range that has been set.

- Never underestimate the time commitment necessary to manage a successful business on one's own. For example, a person who spends forty hours a week focused on his job will have to work considerably more hours as a business owner to fulfil forty hours of activity directly related to providing customers with goods or services. As a result, you will most likely be busier than you have ever been in your life during the early phases of your company.

- It takes many guts to start your own business. Bravery, as the phrase goes, does not pay the bills. You must have more than simple courage to stay in business and be successful. You need much hard work, skill, patience, thorough preparation, and, sometimes, a little luck to be successful.

What do you want to accomplish with your company? How will you know when you've achieved your objective if you want to succeed? What you want to accomplish with your company influences all of the other decisions you will have to make when beginning your entrepreneurial journey. It will influence the kind of company you choose, how you assess your chances of success, and whether or not you possess the requisite skills. Take a look at your resources to determine if you have what it takes to succeed in your new job or business.

3.3 The importance of writing a business plan

Are you thinking of approaching a bank for financial help with your company's operations or growth? If you haven't already done so, the manager will first want to see your business plan. You may not be aware that he will want to view it straight immediately if you haven't already done so.

Perhaps you are not certain that committing the required time and effort to develop a plan is beneficial. If this is the case, the following are the most important benefits for you and your business.

You will never be able to explain your vision for the business as successful as you will be able to do with a well-constructed business plan, no matter how talented a communicator you are. It enables you to understand what you want to achieve clearly. It allows you to present your ideas more concisely.

- Too often, business owners try to present their notions verbally, and at the end of the engagement with the bank, the manager is no wiser than he was at the start of the session. I think you can guess the outcome of many of those requests!
- A business plan can help you persuade both you and the bank of the business's feasibility and viability. Nothing beats having all the facts to help you grasp the most crucial concepts.
- Nothing can hide the fact that a business owner who plans ahead of time seems more ambitious and focused than one who does not. A well-written company plan demonstrates that you have a vision and understand what you want from life and business.
- It's impossible to perceive the hazards or stumbling blocks to achievement when you have so many ideas rushing about in your brain simultaneously. A mind that is overflowing with ideas and possibilities will seldom achieve clarity. A business plan pushes you to arrange your ideas and write them out logically. As a result, you may find yourself on a completely different path than you had expected or decide to abandon your initial idea altogether. Which would you choose, even though it is not a pleasant idea? Is it more vital to lose your hard-earned money or to have the opportunity to reconsider your idea?

It is a wonderful tool for tracking your progress toward the objectives you have set for yourself. By comparing progress to your plan, you will identify whether or not you are deviating from your original vision and what needs to be done to rectify the issue.

Consider the ramifications if you didn't have this precaution: an undetected change in course or a gap in fulfilling your objectives might be disastrous to your company's operations if left unchecked for a long period. But, on the other hand, it may turn out that deviating from your original vision is a better alternative than staying put. In this case, at the very least, admitting the shift allows you to change your course in a planned, structured, and controlled way.

Every action you do has a corresponding impact, and having a plan makes these ramifications clearer. Knowing the probable repercussions of your chosen route allows you to plan and be more prepared to cope with anything the world of self-employment may throw at you. But unfortunately, this is one of the things that "mental planning" cannot do.

Writing down your thoughts may make you recognize that you need to do further market research on the demand for your product or service. It might also mean that you need to do more research on your competitor's products or services. In some cases, more research may be needed to ensure you don't make a mistake that could be very costly. You might even find a previously unknown advantage you didn't know about!

A business plan may assist you in evaluating how much money will be necessary to turn an idea into a reality. You may know how much money you'll need to commit, but until you conduct a cash flow forecast, you may not understand that an overdraft limit and a loan for your equipment will be required to complete the work.

A business plan can help you secure funding. One of the most frequent reasons banks reject loan requests is a lack of information that would enable them to decide on the loan. If the manager does not grasp your idea or business, he will not feel safe enough to assist you. Before he can say yes, he must first comprehend your business. In addition, he may have to explain his decision to give you the money to his superiors in the future, so he needs as much information as possible to back up his decision. A business plan will set his mind at ease and enable him to say yes to more requests in the future.

By the time you finish writing it, you will have a thorough understanding of your company's strengths and weaknesses, the environment in which it operates, what may go wrong, and what you can do to ensure its success. Doing your planning on the back of an envelope will not lead to success in this attempt.

Spend some time writing out your thoughts in a logical and well-organized manner. It will pay you in the long run, both in persuading the bank to take you seriously and preserving your company's future.

4

Chapter 4: Effective Guidelines for Writing a Business Plan

The question is whether or not you are prepared to begin working on your business plan. However, I am certain that you are eager to begin working on your business plan at this moment. Even if this is true for some of you, our technique will be of immense assistance to the great majority of you since it has been used effectively by several entrepreneurs and business plan writers to aid them in developing and building winning business plans. You will learn about what is often included in a business plan in the following chapters, providing you with practical tips and insights and stimulating your thought process by taking you through more than one hundred key questions for business plan writers. You will examine and discuss an example business strategy before concluding. After you have completed reading these chapters in their entirety, you will be well equipped to begin developing your successful business plan for your company.

We hope you have concluded that efficient business planning is necessary for every successful business effort. If you want to raise money, your business plan is the most important collection of documents you will ever submit to a lending institution or prospective investor. It is the most important collection of documents you will ever submit to a lending institution or prospective investor to raise money. Your business plan acts as a road map for your company's journey to financial prosperity. It guides you through every stage of the financing process, allowing you to get to where you want to go faster and more efficiently. First and foremost, it gives you a clear understanding of the steps you must take to achieve your goals and ensure that you are among the businesses that celebrate their fifth anniversary with success and profitability. Your business plan should be complete and realistic to help you reach several important goals, including those below.

It is past time for you to take charge of your professional life. The evidence of your idea is included in the company's strategic strategy. Your ability to focus your efforts on a large project reveals that you have the discipline to achieve success and understand how to bring about development and progress, overcome hurdles along the way, and achieve your final aims. With the aid of your business plan, which will serve as the foundation for your vision, you will be able to turn your ideas into a tangible reality. The development of a master plan is a vital first step. To an entrepreneur, a business plan is similar to a collection of detailed architectural blueprints, similar in scale and complexity to a construction project. An in-depth description of how you will achieve your objectives is provided, with pictures of each step along the way and comparing where you are now and where you want to go. In addition, it will aid you in the preparation or pursuit of an alternative, and perhaps better, course of action. A business plan is a very effective management tool that should be used.

Maintaining open communication lines with team members on your overall approach is critical. The most basic definition of a business plan is a clear statement of purpose that helps you explain to your colleagues how you intend to achieve your goals step-by-step. The business plan may also be used in training and coordination meetings and educating workers about their obligations and accountability for the company to run smoothly. The process of obtaining financial backing for your concept Banks, brokers, investors, prospective partners, and other financial and other resource providers will place a high value on your business plan when selecting whether or not to participate in your venture. Whenever you are looking to hire top-tier employees and financiers, your company plan will act as your initial selling tool, your business résumé, and the beating core of your operation.

It is always necessary to have a professional advisor to help you build your business plan when you expand your company since it will significantly differ from your normal course of business operations. However, it is possible to get various business plan writing services that may be advantageous when starting a small company. Most of these services will be geared toward helping the rising company with its financial, management, and marketing planning needs.

The movement of parameters is required for a business to grow, and the movement must be geared either toward capturing a certain niche or geographic area or toward broadening the company's product offerings. As part of the plan given, a business consultant will often address these problems to guarantee that the entrepreneur is aware of the surrounding environment and the growth trends of the competition, among other things. If you hire a business consultant, they will think about how the project will financially work before giving you advice on how to write a business plan.

Through cash flow management, it is possible to estimate the feasibility of an expansion plan. Depending on the current company's performance, the business consultant may often assist in producing financial projections for the new, bigger business and advising on how to get more funds for the expansion plan. The consultant will also give direction to the client as they go through the process of writing an effective business plan for a growing company. This will include suggestions on how to take advantage of economies of scale. For example, it is important to lower the prices of goods sold in larger quantities while also ensuring that more of these goods are sold, leading to better profits, more sales, or both.

The consultant who will be assisting you through developing your business plan will also discuss other areas of operating a successful company and marketing strategies. For example, marketing consultants and telemarketing consultants are two examples of the services offered in this sector of expertise. To begin with, an evaluation of the state of the economy will be carried out, which will assist in evaluating the purchasing power of the target market. For example, a weakening economy means that the purchasing power of the typical individual declines, and the inverse is also true if an economic boom occurs.

Consequently, the marketing consultant will assist in developing strategies through which marketing campaigns may be used to cultivate long-term customer connections. In addition to providing direction on how to draft a business plan, the consultant will examine the buying trends of the target market, which will aid in the identification of the sorts of commodities or services that the company may offer. In addition, they will analyze how these new commodities might complement the current market's products if they are introduced.

Since the company's development will need less hands-on management and more transfer of responsibility to staff, the business consultant will also give management guidance. Upon completion of the assessment, they will provide suggestions on different management strategies to ensure that service quality remains high when the entrepreneur enters the role of overseer. As a result, the hiring of more managers, the contracting of financial officers and auditors, and the adoption of enterprise resource software will all be required to supervise the functioning of the new, larger company.

4.1 Defining your mission and vision

Incorporate your company's mission statement into a five-hundred-word or less statement that identifies what you will offer and to whom you will sell it and what will motivate customers to buy from you and employees to work for you. Our goal is to help business owners and managers find practical, actionable solutions to problems like marketing, business planning (including forecasting), accounting, and promotion. We also want to use the experience and knowledge of our management team to help our clients grow their businesses.

4.2 Naming your company

Keeping the name short and descriptive is preferable since this will make it easier for people to remember. Be as original as possible, and refrain from employing bombastic or excessive adjectives in your work. Your company's title should be comparable to the headline of a newspaper or magazine story. Describe who you are and what you do under your name and contact information whenever possible. Making people believe what you do is a dangerous marketing tactic that should be avoided. Because your competitor may already have a descriptive and straightforward name, make it simple for yourself and avoid being overly imaginative, which will result in you spending much money to promote a name that does not correspond to the products and services you are providing to the public.

For example, consider the following well-known corporations, all of which have been operating for a long time and which I am all familiar with today: Three of the world's biggest companies are IBM (International Business Machines), AT&T (American Telephone and Telegraph), and General Motors. In addition, IBM, AT&T, and General Motors are three of the world's greatest businesses (GM). While they have grown into other product and service areas since their inception, their names have remained consistent with the products they were originally known for manufacturing: business machines, telephone equipment, and automobiles.

4.3 Your business plan should include

Although how you provide your data to the reader may vary greatly, you should keep the following basic structure of how the business plan should flow in mind:

- A table of contents
- Report Summarization
- Organizational Overview
- Description of the Product and Service
- Market examinations
- The Marketing and Sales Strategy
- Internet Marketing Strategy (if applicable)
- A Strategy for Management and Personnel Development
- Forecasts and predictions
- Appendix

Consequently, I have described the components of a solid business plan that can entice potential investors while also presenting your company with a clear road map that illustrates where you are and where you want to go. But, of course, structure, amount of information, and how fancy and image-oriented things are in your business plan may change based on the purpose of your business plan and the audience for whom it is written.

A cover sheet is included. If you aim to attract prospective investors, money brokers, bankers, venture capitalists, and other possible clients, include a cover page, preferably on company stationery. This will aid you in establishing your effective business plan within a legal framework. Your cover sheet should be as simple as possible. In your cover letter, identify yourself, your company, the institution or party to whom you submit your winning business plan, and the date it will be presented.

Your cover sheet may contain the following items:

- Information about your company, which may include:
- The company's full legal name
- The company's address (street, city, state, zip/postcode)
- Telephone numbers
- The main points of contact, or a group of contacts, together with their titles
- A brief business paragraph that gives a promotional overview of your company's goals, potential, and prospects
- The amount of money you need now and in the future
- Whenever possible, provide the name or names of someone who has recommended you to the investment source.

The table of contents is as follows: You are organized, precise, and attentive to the needs of the people you are contacting will speak volumes about you to your possible lender. If your potential lender knows the road plan you're providing to him, you'll seem to be able to manage the big picture. How many books have you opened or read that didn't have a table of contents to begin with? Most of us start there when we want to get a basic feel of what the book is about. We recommend that you write the table of contents last and use specific page numbers in your document

The key points are summarized: This is the one portion of your business plan that everyone who looks at it will read thoroughly before advancing. When presenting a business plan to a customer, this part must catch and hold the client's attention throughout the process. Examine if it can be read in a few minutes or less. Make it interesting to pique the reader's interest! When readers lose interest in your business plan, they will put it down and go to the next one.

The executive summary condenses the whole of your business plan into the shortest possible statement about the nature and goals of your business in just a few lines. First, identify the most important ideas you want to express to the financing source in each business plan component, beginning with your company overview and finishing with your appendices. Then, keep it short and sweet, with two to five pages of written content.

Keep in mind that this summary is a condensed and readily digested version of the whole company plan. So don't skip over this section since it will show that you can focus with precision on your aims and explain clearly that you understand who you are, what you want, and where you want to go.

A company's synopsis will include information about your business in this section, such as who you are, where you have been, where you want to go, and how your company fits into your sector and marketplace. In addition, you will submit information about your goods and services.

Suppose you can offer a comprehensive overview of the industry in which your business operates. In that case, it will be easier to demonstrate how your company fits into the bigger picture of the industry in which it operates. This will boost your company's confidence in its capacity to fulfil its goals. You will identify and argue the following points in this section:

- The particulars of your company's activities
- A brief history of the company, as well as how its products and services were developed,
- How do your existing facilities support future growth?
- Understanding your company's organizational features is critical, especially its legal framework.
- It will be looked at to make your company's products and services more appealing to the general public by looking at recently announced things.

4.4 Positive economic trends

Any contracts or agreements that say that business and money will come in the future are legally binding. This information, along with any other relevant information you may like to provide, serves as the foundation for your company's profile. In addition, this section should give the reader insight into how your company functions and why it has a strong chance of succeeding in the market.

In product and service descriptions you will specifically describe what you make or what service you provide, how you make or provide the product, and whether you intend to expand your business by offering new and better products and services that will result in increased revenues and a higher bottom-line profit for the investment source.

When composing this section, thoroughly describe your products and services so that the investment source understands what you're attempting to offer them. A company can only get loans and investments if the lenders and investors think its strategy has been well thought out, examined, and planned.

Analysis and investigation of the market as previously stated in this chapter, you will be describing to the funding source the present market in which you want to operate your company. You will also go through your company plan with the finance provider. When deciding which market to target with your products and services, think about the attributes of your goods and services, the lifestyle of your customers, where they live, and, if necessary, the time of year.

The quantity of research: The research you do on your target market when developing a profile of that market will affect the quality of your analysis. Your neighbourhood library and the phone will be two of your most effective friends. Use them to their full capacity! Use the information and data available in books, directories, and case studies to help you make educated judgments.

Prospective investors will be blown away by your comprehensive inquiry in ways you can't even conceive. Use your time wisely while you're here. Be thorough in your research while creating this market profile. Show that you finished your studies with attentive attention to detail and dedication.

Creating a Marketing and Sales Plan: As I mentioned previously in this chapter, marketing strategy may be described as the science of designing and conducting promotional campaigns to generate sales for your company. You want them to talk about the good things about your products or services. They should also try to get people to want to buy your products or services.

When evaluating your options: Consider that the bulk of the approaches available to you will need financial investment and that each one will target a different demographic. A marketing strategy that enables you to reach the most significant number of people possible while spending the least money possible is essential. To avoid flushing money down the toilet, it is critical that you spend time investigating which marketing techniques may be most appropriate for your company and its products and services. As previously stated, wasting money on the wrong marketing strategies is equivalent to flushing money down the toilet.

The following is a solid recommendation: Keep track of your expenditures in each area and your results. If a specific place provides a significant advantage, you may wish to raise your spending in that area, and if no response occurs in another area, you may want to cut your spending in that region. If you do not keep track of your outcomes, you will never be able to determine what works and what does not work. We believe you would prefer that the money stayed in your pocket rather than being flushed down the toilet.

The internet is the focus of this strategy: If your company sells products and services over the Internet, or if it plans to do so in the future, you must carefully plan a cost-effective strategy that will maximize your reach to your target audience. You may already know the advantages and disadvantages of conducting business over the Internet and the most efficient methods of achieving the results you require with the least amount of money spent for those new to this field. However, if you are new to this field, you may not be aware of the advantages and disadvantages of conducting business over the Internet and the most efficient methods of achieving the results you require with the least amount of money spent. If you don't know how to build an Internet strategy that will get the best results, I strongly suggest you research and talk to people who know a lot about the subject.

Selling on eBay: Purchasing a domain name, creating a website with various items for sale, taking payments via PayPal, or setting up your credit card gateway and payment processing system are all possibilities. Any way you choose to get money for a project, do your research and make it clear what you want to do. This way, the source of the money doesn't have to guess what you want to do.

Management and human resource strategies should be developed: Those considering investing in a business place a high degree of importance on the team of executives who will make critical day-to-day decisions for the business. It will be up to you and your partners and the board of directors and management team that you have put together to see if your business succeeds or fails.

When it comes to creating a great business plan: It is vital that you and your management team completely understand every word, every line, and every component of the plan before presenting it to a possible investor for consideration. A thorough description of your road map to success might considerably improve your prospects of obtaining the financing or investment capital you need. Moreover, knowing that your management team will be travelling on the same bus as you and will arrive at the same location will provide you with an additional piece of mind throughout your trip. Taking these steps will help you achieve the goals you have set out in your company's plan.

Budgetary estimates and projections are also included: These are the building blocks of your business plan—the point at which your vision is described in terms of dollars and cents, as well as time units such as days, weeks, months, and years—and they serve as the basis for your strategy since they are the starting point for your company plan. Every one of the investment sources that will be assessing your proposal will thoroughly examine your financial projections and forecasts. Your financial predictions should be broken down into monthly projections for the first two years and then into annual projections for the next two years and beyond. As a bonus, you may include annual summary pages for each of the years in your forecasts so that the reader can get a quick overview of what you are projecting. Financial projections should be included in your plan for at least three years; however, the total number of years may differ depending on the type of business you currently manage or wish to start and your industry.

Describe the resources required: For example, if you use your business plan to get necessary resources from lenders or investors, this part will detail your precise requirements—including the amount, conditions, and date of need—and how the resources will be used to further your company objectives. Finally, you will include how the money will be repaid to the lender in your cash flow forecasts if you get funding. Specifically, in the case of a capitalization that includes equity partners, your projections will indicate the increase in equity and an estimated schedule for distributing profits among the partners.

Appendix depending on your business plan: Any or all of the following aspects may be included in this section to provide additional relevant information about the financing source while also supporting the disclosures made throughout your business plan.

5

Chapter 5: Writing a Business Plan

This chapter walks you through creating a well-written professional business plan, step by step. A well-written professional business plan may assist you in beginning your company, obtaining financing, and expanding your business. When it comes to drafting a company plan, it is not required to be sophisticated. To put together a successful corporate plan, it is not required to have a business or accounting degree. Instead, business planning may be straightforward—and even entertaining in certain cases! By reading this chapter, you will learn how to finish your plan with the least amount of hassle and annoyance. Once you have finished this course, you will be better prepared to start, run, and grow your business.

5.1 Organizational structure and function

The value of understanding where you are right now, where you've been, and where you wish to go is not immediately apparent. This is quite important. Potential lenders and investment groups will want to know that you have a deep understanding of the industry in which your business operates and your company's strengths, weaknesses, and long-term aspirations and plans. Although you are a well-established corporation with years of experience behind you, it may be easier for you to comprehend the path you are taking. However, how can you tell whether you are on the right track? What is your vision for your company if you are a new business startup looking to take it to the next level? Do you know where you want to take it and how you plan to get there? True or false, you have undertaken a substantial amount of study to guarantee that your assumptions are valid. Are you thinking of launching a new business? Take some time to think about where you have personally been in your business career.

Do you feel sure that the lessons you have learned will help you and your company go in the direction you want? As a result of our many years of experience working with business owners and managers, I have yet to meet a business owner who did not alter their company's view due to producing an effective, winning business plan for their business. Those businesses that have been in operation for a long period would benefit from the information provided. After completing the process, they would be able to tell anyone in two minutes who they were and what they did, where they were based and how they operated their company.

After inquiring about someone's profession, how often have you discovered that they cannot describe what they do due to their inability to communicate effectively? According to them, they are attorneys. Wonderful! This reveals a great deal to me! You must ask them twenty questions to better understand what they do daily. Do you own and manage your own company? Describe the areas of the law in which you have a special interest. Have you been putting your abilities to the test for some time now? Wouldn't it have been nice if the person had given you what is known in business networking as an elevator speech (a two-minute presentation)? Wouldn't that have been lovely?

Making a full understanding of your company before talking about it with anybody, especially lenders and investment sources, will ensure that they are happy to know what you are talking about when crafting a successful business plan. Include the following information in this section of your business plan: the company's name, when and by whom it was founded, its legal structure, its mission and vision statements, its current situation, goals and objectives, and any other issues or items that you believe are important to communicate about the company when putting together this section of your business plan: Your company's mission statement should encapsulate the essence of what the company stands for, including its fundamental values, purpose, and strategic direction, among other things. When it comes to your company's vision statement, it should be succinct and compelling to inspire and motivate everyone who works there. If you believe your company will be in a certain position at some point in the future, your vision statement should explain that position clearly and simply.

Prepare your replies carefully and thoroughly, ensuring that all pertinent information is included in your winning business plan and that your responses have been well-thought-out, researched, and addressed exhaustively. It is vital, in my opinion, to underline how critical this procedure is. Because your thoughts, ideas, and views change as you write a business plan, you must go back over your written content. Is it too much for you to handle right now? It is conceivable. Will it take an extended period to complete? Without a doubt, the answer is yes. The most crucial question is whether or not it will result in improved results. The answer to this question is an emphatic yes. To think beyond the box, it is vital that you challenge your thinking and stimulate your creativity. Your activities will likely increase your chances of reaching the goals and objectives you have set out before. We regularly discuss this subject with new business start-ups and existing business owners when I meet with them.

After a while, and as I get further along in the process of establishing the plan, individuals begin to view things differently and in a more comprehensible manner, which results in the production of new ideas and concepts as well as new directions that are beneficial to the business as a whole. Having a friend or family member experienced in the business world and asking them to analyze these questions with you may be valuable in advancing your company's idea. Request his assistance in questioning your preconceived notions and developing a more comprehensive picture of where you are, where you want to be, and how you plan to get there. Apart from being well-versed in your company's operations, it is vital that you be capable of explaining the core of your business in a succinct, clear, and concise manner to those who are unfamiliar with your business's operations. When you meet with an investor or lender, make sure you don't come across as if you're a deer caught in the headlights.

Consider the case of a successful client who approached us for help in preparing a business plan to get a $50,000 credit line to expand his company. While I had our first discussion, he informed us that he had visited his bank and that they were hesitant about the direction he wanted to take his company. However, they were not persuaded to provide him with the line of credit he asked for, even though he had good credit standing with them before his application. Instead, they recommended that he put up a company plan and show it to them within the next four days. Developing a successful business plan with our customers allowed us to revise several areas of the plan and create a road map that was both clear and concise. On top of all that, our client, who had assumed he knew everything about his company, learned that there was much more to learn, which he promptly did. In the following weeks, our client went to his bank and was approved for a $50,000 credit line, which he had previously refused due to his lack of presentation skills. We are quite delighted that this client was able to grow his company and then sell it for a considerable quantity of money many years later.

5.2 An explanation of your product and service

Your goods or services may seem uninteresting to investors and lenders, especially if they are conventional commodities. However, investors and lenders are concerned with much more than a basic description of your products or services when making investment or lending decisions. Beginning with your location, where your products and services are procured, how you obtain them, and at what price, where and how you start manufacturing and inventorying them, how much you charge for them, how visitors distribute and deliver them, and how you manage your workplace and cash flow throughout the process should all be included. Many entrepreneurs start a business because they feel that no one else can produce a widget as excellent as theirs. This has been our observation throughout the years.

They were probably true in some circumstances, but it seems not in all of them. In terms of operating a business, the only problem is that there is much more to it than just producing widgets. If this applies to you, you should be aware of the phrase "Entrepreneur, beware!". Prepare your replies carefully and thoroughly, ensuring that all pertinent information is included in your winning business plan and that your responses have been well-thought-out, researched, and addressed exhaustively. To maximize the profitability of your products and services, it is vital that you understand the processes that must be followed from beginning to end, from beginning to end, and from beginning to end. Unless you do so, investors and lenders will be wary of lending your money because you lack trust in your ability to communicate effectively with them.

For example, after examining his inventory and purchasing procedures, I had a successful client growing quickly and needed more finances to pay for inventory purchases. I discovered that he lost valuable production time while waiting for raw materials to arrive. As a result, he was paying much more for the same things than other businesses in the same industry. We developed a program with one of his primary suppliers that assured supplies were delivered on time and at a lower price than others in the same industry were paying for each item purchased. After learning about our client's arrangement with his vendor and how he was able to boost productivity while contributing more money to the bottom line, the lender was delighted to grant him the credit line increase he had requested. Our client's business has grown a lot over the years, and he now runs a very profitable business, which I am happy to report.

5.3 Market research and analysis

It is important that your willingness to investigate, evaluate, and explore your market to analyse it. This is quite important. Even if your company is a start-up or an established corporation, prospective lenders and investment groups will assess the potential of your market and decide whether or not you will be able to conduct a successful business in that market. You have done research in this area will be clear to them, so make sure you have done it. There is no room for rushing when you write an effective business plan. Most business owners assume they have a great understanding of their sector, which may be true. However, have you undertaken rigorous market research on your own company's products and services? If you haven't already, jump right in and start the process because you may be surprised at how much you discover about your target market and what your competitors are all about due to your research. Individuals who have just started or want to start a business would be wise to do extensive market research at this time.

You will gain valuable knowledge by researching, analyzing, and assessing your market. This information will assist you in developing marketing and sales strategies that will provide the greatest return on your investment dollars. Providing the necessary information to investors and lenders is essential. While developing a profile of your target market, it is vital to keep in mind that the quality of your research will influence the strength of the analysis you do. Developing a target market profile is a key step in developing a marketing strategy. While working on this project, it is critical that you make good use of your time and resources. You may find that your local library and chamber of commerce, the Internet and telephone, and marketing professionals are some of your most successful partners. To the greatest extent possible, make the most of them! Use existing resources such as books, directories, case studies, and the Internet to obtain knowledge and data for

44

your project. If you do a thorough investigation, prospective investors will be more impressed than you think, so take your time putting up this market description.

Make a strong case for yourself by demonstrating that you finished your studies with painstaking attention to detail and appropriate commitment. Make the most of your available time. To be successful, you must first determine your target audience and location. Consumers of your products and services and their geographical area must be properly defined, and I don't simply mean in broad terms. Identifying your customers and their geographic location is critical.

You should include information on individual customers in your data results, including information on your market's overall demographic scope and your market's overall demographic scope split down by gender and age. In addition, other demographic information, such as marital status, family size, the number of homeowners vs renters, income per person and household, and income by gender, should be provided. Also necessary is a thorough examination of their purchasing and spending habits as they pertain to personal items such as clothing and household goods, social activities such as dining out and watching movies, work expenses such as uniforms and office supplies, vacation activities such as weekend trips and cruises, relaxation activities such as reading books and magazines or watching television while sipping a beverage, and luxury items such as boats and fancy cars, among other things.

You must understand what makes your target market tick and what pushes them to spend their hard-earned money. An essential component of your business plan is identifying your target area or areas and explaining how the demographics of the target area will be sufficient for you to achieve the goals and objectives you have set for yourself. You must consider the geographic scope of your target market, as defined above, the type and size of the business you are selling to, the number of employees they have, and the number of years they have been in business, among other factors. You must also consider their purchasing and spending habits and the type and size of the business they are selling to. If they are already buying or planning to purchase what you are giving, you will need to determine how much they have already spent and what they expect to spend. Most crucially, you will need to determine how much they intend to spend.

When doing significant market research, evaluating, and researching, you should seriously consider opting not to build your business, at least not in that specific target market, since the market will not be adequate to maintain your company's operations. For example, suppose you are currently in business and have realized that your target market is insufficient to fund your operation. In that case, you may want to examine other products or services that you may provide; your market will support that. In addition, you may wish to investigate if it is feasible to extend your market's size and geographic location.

Alternately, you may want to consider developing an exit strategy to depart the company. It is essential if you want to be successful in business that you are aware of the identities and locations of your competitors, as well as what they are doing to win market share. The names of rivals, their locations, the techniques they use to sell their goods and services, the amount of market share each has, and whether or not any new competitors may be anticipated or predicted are all important factors to consider while investigating your particular target market. This stage must be completed regardless of whether you sell to individual or corporate clients. You must discover all you can about your opponent that you possibly can find out about them, and there are several ways to do so, as described below.

If your target market is large enough, several ways to identify who and where your competitors are situated may be utilized to narrow down the list of potential competitors. To learn more about them, you may use resources such as trade publications, directories, and magazines in your profession, the yellow pages, online business directories, or simply by walking or driving around your target market region. You should make certain that every one of your competitors is characterized, including any organizations competing for the same purchasing dollar as you are. For example, pretend you're in the following situation: You'd want to open your sandwich shop. Even though your first reaction may be to focus only on sandwich shops directly competing with one another, you shouldn't restrict your search to just those firms. You should also think about whether there are any other restaurants where a consumer might buy a meal for around the same price as you are charging and have it delivered for the same length of time as you are offering.

Companies that provide hamburgers, chicken sandwiches, salads served buffet-style, and pizza, for example, may suit your requirements since you and these other businesses are all competing for the same purchasing dollar. The food court of a large shopping mall is an excellent example. What should you do when you're presented with anything from six to ten companies all fighting for your attention and urging you to join their queue and make a purchase from them? What should you do? Walking around each of them and looking at the food they are serving, you will almost always end up in line at the store with the best food presentation, which will also be the business with the longest line, unless you have an aversion to anything in particular. (Unless you are in a huge hurry, you will go to the front of the line and then be disappointed after you have done eating).

Afterwards, after you've discovered who your competitors are, you'll need to find out what they're doing to attract new customers. Among the alternatives are the following: Other options include shopping for them or having someone you know shop for you, standing outside their place of business and monitoring traffic flow, and a variety of other approaches. To be successful, you must first determine what they are doing to be successful. The more you know about them, the better you can develop marketing and sales strategies that will help you compete with them and get closer to getting your desired market share.

5.4 Marketing and sales plan

Many entrepreneurs who put up their business plans may assume that all they want to do is open the doors of their company and start selling, rather than first constructing a full marketing and sales strategy to back up their efforts. You should avoid going into meetings with investors and lenders in this state of mind because you will be turned away and forced to walk out the door. It should be obvious to them, as it should be to you by now, how vital it is for every component of your business strategy to be successful. When it comes to business, the difference between making money and losing money comes down to following your conscience rather than doing what you want or know how to do to achieve your goals. If you want to lose yours, then do it.

On the other hand, investors and lenders are anxious about the safety of their investments from being stolen or lost. Our primary point here is that while establishing your marketing and sales strategies, you must consider all of the components of your marketing and sales strategies that I have explored so far in this chapter. You may have amazing success with certain things, but others may not go as smoothly as you hoped. You must examine the likelihood of success when developing a great marketing mix and use the best channels and approaches that may increase brand recognition while also generating revenue to be successful. To be more specific, they are two of the most critical goals to attain while designing marketing and sales campaigns. Even with well-considered strategies, trial and error will be part of the learning process while acquiring a new skill or technique.

This makes it even more important to keep track of where your money is going and what kind of return you are obtaining from it. One of our successful customers spent $8,000 per month on four different advertising mailers that four different suppliers were producing. He was really happy with the results he was receiving. We asked him to focus on his advertising budget during our interview and which mailer was the most effective at bringing in new customers. His inability to respond was because he did not have a tracking system. We stressed the need to closely monitor his advertising expenses to guarantee that he was earning a reasonable return on his advertising investment. He agreed. Six months after building and installing a monitoring system, he discovered that one of the mailers, the most expensive at $4,000 per month, was not even paying its expenses since it was producing less than $3,000 per month in revenue. He immediately discontinued the mailer.

Our client decided to discontinue the mailer's use and begin testing with a new one that was far less costly and that began to pay for itself within the first three months of operation. This is a fantastic example of how to prevent squandering your money in the future. In addition, I am glad to inform you that the company's revenue has increased dramatically over the preceding two years, with a promising forecast for the future.

5.5 Personnel development and management strategy

The first significant heading in this section of your successful business plan should be "Management and Personnel Plan" or "Management," depending on your personal taste. After that, you should describe why and by whom the company was founded and any other significant information you feel is essential to the reader. Financial projections, marketing tactics, and even the most innovative product or service to provide to the world will be rendered useless if your company's management staff is not strong and equipped with the necessary competence to steer it to success. Your company's management team has the power to either build or break the business.

Unlike anybody else, this group should be able to advertise your company's concept more successfully than any other. Provide the very minimum of information about your team as soon as possible. In this section, you may find information on how much relevant knowledge your team has, how many years of marketing experience the team has, the kind of essential employees the business employs, who the company's founders are and what they own, and other similar information. Is your team fully staffed, or do you have any gaps to be closed? Do you have faith in your capabilities? If you answered yes, do you have a well-defined organizational structure, complete with job descriptions and clear responsibilities for all key members?

The likelihood that you will not have the whole team available while drafting the business plan is high, particularly true for start-up companies. You should make it a point to identify any gaps or weaknesses in your company's operations and how you intend to fix any gaps or weaknesses in the future. It is possible that including extra resources which are not on your payroll as part of your team may be a beneficial solution to this problem (especially if you are just starting as a one-person show). Keep in touch with professionals such as your attorney, accountant, outside consultants, insurance agent, and even a board of directors. Building an advisory board, or better yet, a board of directors willing to act as a sounding board for you and support your decision-making as you grow your company, maybe advantageous when seeking finance. You should also go into as much detail as possible about how your management team is equipped to lead your company to the next level of success. Discuss your team members' experience and areas of expertise and how they connect to the company's requirements. Discussion topics include:

5.5.1 Predicting and forecasting your finance

Finally, but certainly not least, there is the chapter on your financial plan to consider. Even though this is the most challenging component of launching a company, the process need not be as complicated or time-consuming as it seems at first. For the most part, corporate financials for startups are less complex than you may expect, and a business degree is certainly not required to design a strong financial strategy for a company. However, to be clear, if you want more support, several tools and resources are available to assist you in establishing a solid financial plan.

In most cases, the following components will be included in a financial plan:

- For the first 12 months, monthly sales and revenue estimates will be provided. Yearly projections for the following three to five years will then be provided. Forecasts for the next three years are normally acceptable, while some investors may insist on a five-year prediction in particular situations.
- It is the location where all of your data comes together to illustrate whether or not you are making a profit or a loss in accounting, and it is also known as a profit and loss statement (or P&L).
- In finance, a cash flow statement is a financial statement that indicates how much money is coming in and leaving out at any given time. So, although your profits and losses are computed on your company's income statement, the cash flow statement keeps track of how much cash (money in the bank) you have on hand at any given moment.
- A balance sheet summarizes a corporation's assets, liabilities, and equity-like a financial statement. It gives you a quick and simple look at the financial health of your business.
- If you seek investors' financial assistance, you should include a brief section in your business plan detailing how you intend to spend their cash. A common phrase used in this context is "use of funds."

You should also offer a concise description of your exit strategy, which will interest investors. It is important to have an exit strategy in place if you ever decide to sell your business, whether to another company or the broader public, via an initial public offering (IPO). Any potential investors who may be interested in hearing your thoughts on this topic will contact you. On the other hand, leaving out the exit strategy portion of your business plan is acceptable if you are running a company that you want to keep under your control indefinitely and are not seeking angel or venture capital investment.

Expert accountants should seek professional advice and help if they have never studied a financial statement in the past and are worried and bewildered about how and where to begin. Be mindful of the importance of thoroughly understanding the information contained in your financial statements and projections, including a profit and loss statement, balance sheet, cash flow statement, use of proceeds table, or written statement, as well as the assumptions that were used, regardless of whether they were developed by you or someone else.

Check that they walk you through each line item, step by step, repeatedly, until you have a thorough understanding of how and why they function. It would be inappropriate to position oneself in front of investors or lenders if you did not have this level of knowledge. You and they will both be wasting your and their time if you do this. It takes a great deal of time and effort to compile and assess financial statements and the documentation, but these records are also essential management tools. The introduction to us of one of our successful customers came about because he was experiencing financial troubles. His company was always months behind schedule in compiling financial statements and addressing significant balance sheet concerns. The owner couldn't have cared less since he thought it made little difference to the bottom line.

Over several months, our collaboration with his company's accounting department resulted in the successful implementation of a system that allowed them to create and produce timely and accurate financial statements and support analysis for all items on the balance sheet and profit and loss statement. During the course of the process, they were able to determine how much cash was being kept in accounts receivable and inventory and identify areas where money was being squandered on products that were not needed. Soon after they started cutting down in these areas, money began to flow into their bank account like a river. We are glad to inform you that our client's growth has continued over the preceding three years, including new people and new product offers. We want to thank everyone who has contributed to this success.

5.5.2 Executive summary report

When writing an executive summary, one of the essential aims is to provide the reader with an interesting and exciting overview of your company's activities. This is accomplished by presenting them with a summary of each section of your plan. The body of the summary incorporates the most interesting points you made over the plan's construction. The "sizzle" of your company's plan must be included in your executive summary. If you do not immediately capture the investor or lender's attention, you will likely not do so later.

If you think that any sections of your business plan need to be changed to give it more oomph, go back and modify those areas of your plan as necessary. To decide if your executive summary captures the attention of business partners, family members, and friends, I propose that you have them read it to see whether it is simple to grasp. If not, go back and add a bit more spice to it while also clarifying any confusing or unclear areas that may have appeared.

5.5.3 Appendix

A list of all of the backup papers that include or support the material that you have previously supplied should be included in the appendix section of your work. You will be required to supply any supporting documents important to your case for your winning business plan, and all of the facts, statements, and claims to be considered valid. Depending on your needs, your most important information may be gathered from various sources, including the Internet, the library, industry magazines and publications, and even your customers and competitors. Using the Internet, you may access several search engines, which you can use to get started searching for whatever information you are seeking.

We hope you find these of assistance. Likely, your local public library has previously published papers, publications, bulletins, research and statistics and other resources that may be of use to you in identifying and validating your claims, among other things. Additional figures from market surveys done by an impartial surveying company should be sought after. A significant amount of this material, which includes industrial magazines and publications, may usually be found in the reference area of the library's reference department, located on the second floor. Your most loyal customers may prove to be your most powerful allies when it comes to authenticating the quality of your products and services and the overall character of your business. Suppose you can persuade loyal, satisfied customers and respected community members to provide you with a letter of recommendation. In that case, you will be light years ahead of your competition in terms of credibility and reputation. Try to persuade them to write their letters of recommendation on the company's letterhead to the extent possible. Depending on the scenario, it may be necessary to personally shop your competitors or engage someone to do so on your behalf to back up any claims you make about your competitors.

As much written information as you can obtain from them, including product brochures, pricing information, and information on lead times, how long they have been in business, and what they feel sets them apart from their competition, is essential (if they have anything). Always keep in mind that, to compete, you must first comprehend who and what you are up against to succeed.

6

Chapter 6: Putting Your Business Plan into Action

If you follow a basic approach and build an adequate structure for your company's business plan, the process of writing, researching, assembling, revising, and rewriting a successful business plan may be tremendously satisfying. Beyond that, and this is critical, a recorded business plan will serve as the vehicle through which you will be able to get the capital you will need to start or expand your company.

A potential investor or lender may have made the following comment to you: "I'm sorry, but before I can make a decision, I'd want to see your business plan." In today's environment, if you are looking for outside funding for your company or idea, a business plan is now just as vital as having a business card and an email address to attract the attention of investors. Determine that you must spend all of your time and energy building a more successful business plan to create excitement about your project and, ultimately, convince investors or bankers to believe in your company or idea and offer financial assistance in support of that confidence.

Without specific instructions on implementing the plan, even the most well-thought-out company strategy is nothing more than a piece of paper with no real substance behind it. In the implementation plan section of your business plan, you will accomplish the following tasks:

- Make your objectives very clear.
- Assign tasks to your team members that have deadlines attached to them.
- Continue to keep tabs on your progress toward attaining your goals and reaching milestones.
- Each one of these initiatives will serve as a foundation for the growth and development of your business

6.1 Clearly stating your goals is essential

Because your objectives will serve as the basis for the rest of your implementation plan, it is critical that they be crystal clear and precisely stated. For example, consider the following scenario: Your business is a tiny consulting company that has just launched. If you want to be successful, you should choose a goal that is both tough and feasible. For example, it may look like this:

- In three months, you will have obtained office space and be ready to begin operations for your company.
- During the first three months of your company's existence, sign up three new consumers for your services.
- Obtain a total of 10 new customers throughout the first year of business.
- Formulating proper goals and objectives for implementing your company's strategy will drive you to show up and perform daily, thus increasing your productivity.
- If you don't set goals that motivate you to improve daily, it's easy to get stagnant in your business and just float about doing a barely sufficient job for the rest of your life. For your aspirations and ideas to become a

reality, you must first determine what they are.

6.2 Break down the work into smaller parts

It is necessary to accomplish the tasks listed in this area of your company's implementation plan to achieve the overall goals and objectives listed in the plan. Include a task manager at each stage to ensure that responsibilities are clearly defined and maintain accountability.

Important to remember is that while you're generating well-defined tasks and assignments for yourself, the descriptions should be basic and general; do not go into detail about how the activities will be carried out in a step-by-step, micromanaged manner. Alternately, concentrate on the expected consequences associated with the responsibilities in question. If I go with the prior example, the tasks section of your implementation plan will look something like this:

- A safe office location to work from.
- You must get all the necessary licenses and permits.
- The office manager should be in charge of setting up the phones and computers.
- Customers should be recruited as soon as possible by the sales manager.
- The development of marketing materials is the responsibility of the marketing manager.
- A client's suggestion should be requested, and the relationship manager should do so.

This list is very specific to this particular company and is intended to be used just as a fast indicator of the company's capabilities. Make your life easier by going into more detail and assigning tasks to yourself, such as getting money and meeting new people, to make it easier.

6.3 Scheduling your time

A reasonable time frame for completion must support each item in your implementation plan to determine whether or not your plan is practicable. Certain tasks will undoubtedly take longer to complete than others; therefore, make every effort to establish appropriate time estimates.

It is your job to do the research, find instructional resources that will help you through the implementation process, or look for a partner, mentor, or contractor with more experience who can help you implement your plan.

While being proactive while still being suitable with your time allocation can ensure completion and high-quality work, you should avoid being too pushy in your time management. Instead, use time-management tools such as Microsoft Project or create your own Gantt chart to assist you in organizing this schedule. Creating a Gantt chart is a valuable tool for visualizing how long it will take to complete certain activities and what sequence should be finished.

6.4 The process for progress

To make sure your business plan is done on time and within budget, you or a member of your management team must keep track of the progress of each action and the percentage of each goal that has been met.

When delays do occur, however, make every attempt to identify and resolve the root of the problem. Is it feasible that the person in charge made a clumsy move and dropped the ball? A significant number of tasks were placed on their shoulders. Does this raise the possibility of legal action if a third party, such as a supplier or bank, fails to perform its responsibilities under a contract? Make the appropriate revisions to your Gantt chart to account for the delay. Take note of the previous deadline and the reason why it didn't meet its completion requirement, as well.

Compared to the later stages of a startup's growth, the procedures described above are important in the early stages since it is during this era that sound management habits are created and because it is also during this period that money has not yet started to flow. Therefore, increasing the effectiveness with which you begin implementing your company plan increases your chances of surviving this vital period.

7

Chapter 7: Improving Customer Relationship

In every company, the client is an essential stakeholder to consider. The capacity of a company to attract and keep customers is critical to its long-term survival, growth, and profitability. As a result, the expression "the customer is king" came to be. Therefore, client relationships are an inescapable stumbling block when implementing any company plan. Understanding the link or affiliation between a company and its customers is vital to comprehending customer relationships. Client retention, expansion, and acquisition are all decided by how the business acquires, keeps, and grows these customers. Developing strong, therefore, developing customer connections.

Customers will continue to return and suggest others, resulting in a rise in customer loyalty, greater brand awareness, and an increase in sales. The objective of every business should always be to have a favourable connection with its customers. It is vital to have a well-defined plan for gaining clients for a company, maintaining those customers, managing them, and expanding the client base to succeed. The way a company approaches and solves this critical slice of any business model canvas directly influences the company's launch, survival, development, and profitability under consideration. It is necessary to consider several critical factors that determine the character of business-customer interactions. The following are some of these considerations:

Based on the characteristics of the connection that the customer seeks to have with the company, the client's expectations are segmented. This is the result of things like how the situation is set up, what kind of customer service is expected, and the general nature of the relationship, to name a few.

- The client relationships that have already been created are still in effect.
- The business's size is measured in square feet.
- The cost of running and maintaining these partnerships is a separate line item on the balance sheet.
- Which methods are the most successful for incorporating them into the business model?

It is possible to establish client relationships in several ways, including via personalized services such as automated customer support, self-service, and segmented service, among other methods.

As a result, the following key customer relationship components must be appropriately handled in managing client expectations:

- What techniques do you use to draw in new customers?
- What strategies do you use to manage and maintain them?
- What measures do you use to retain and grow these customers?
- The issue is, how can you attract clients to your company?

Instead of seeing customers as passive recipients of services, it is vital to consider them as people with views continuously, needs they want to have satisfied, and issues they wish to have handled. Therefore, your product should aim to fulfil the wants and expectations of your consumers and provide solutions to their problems, thus adding value to their lives in the process.

START WITH A BUSINESS PLAN

When you have comprehensive knowledge of your customer, you can generate more value more effectively. If you want to do a good job filling in the business model canvas, you should think about the following things:

- What marketing technique would the business use to attract its initial customers?
- What methods would get people to know about the company and its products?
- People think about these things when they decide whether or not to buy a product.
- What procedures must be followed to make the first purchase and ensure that the product continues to function correctly after being purchased?

According to this "essential" question, it is "important" to identify and understand the customers' thoughts, visions, feelings, and behaviours and how they affect the company and its products. Therefore, you should make an effort to get to know your customers, including current and future customers.

7.1 Establishing prospective client's relationship

Because consumers' interests might vary based on the type of company, it is vital to establish who the targeted customers are and what they want before developing a strategy for reaching them. Consequently, it is always important to recognize them and consider their diversity and homogeneity. When deciding whether to segment the market in the first place, this will help make a choice. When it comes to marketing, customer segmentation refers to breaking customers into similar groups based on particular traits that they all have in common.

In addition to providing a more full and deep understanding of your consumers, creating customer segments also provides a better understanding of what is important to them individually and what solutions they seek.

As a consequence, there is a greater possibility of value addition occurring. Consumers should be looked at for the following things during the process of getting to know them:

This is the problem that has to be addressed. In every business model creation process, identifying the problem that your business model will aim to solve is crucial at the beginning of the process. It is meaningless to provide a solution to a problem that does not exist. Because the scale of a problem is greater, customers are more likely to respond positively to the solutions that your business strives to provide. Businesses must do market research and feasibility studies to understand their customers better and determine how to attract them to their products or services. They must also be aware of the problems that their customers are having, and they must come up with meaningful and cost-effective solutions to those problems.

Budgets and the willingness of customers to pay for the items are both key factors to consider when making purchasing decisions. Questions such as the following are samples of those that must be answered:

- Buyers are eager to pay the total price for the goods, but are they able to?
- Which groups are more likely to be the most generous payers for clients?
- What is the pricing range they are willing to accept for this product?
- How much money will be spent to make the product more user-friendly?
- What percentage of a premium are customers ready to pay for this level of customization, and how much money are they willing to spend on this level of customization?

When a solution is acceptable and focused on solving a specific issue, the chances of people desiring to purchase the product improve dramatically. For example, customers' needs and expectations may change depending on the industry they are engaged in. Therefore, it is essential to think about how flexible the product is and how much it will cost to meet the needs of specific groups of customers when you are making a new product.

Customers' ability to contact them regularly. Consumers have legitimate worries about their accessibility, and they are well-founded. However, customers must be convinced that they can be contacted with relative ease or difficulty and that contacting them will not be prohibitively expensive before they agree to participate. It is impossible to overstate the necessity of doing a cost-benefit analysis. Given that the primary purpose of a business is to make a profit, the cost of getting a customer must not be more than the value derived from acquiring the customer in the first place.

One of the most important goals is to obtain the customer at the lowest possible cost. Also necessary is a thorough and balanced evaluation of customer acquisitions. While it may appear to be more expensive in the short term to obtain certain customers, it may become more profitable in the long run for a variety of strategic reasons or simply because it is more profitable. In certain cases, incurring more costs now rather than later may be considered a "well-justified sacrifice." Think about the following things while making your decision:

The desired market share is the magnitude of the anticipated market share in percentage terms. The company's target market influences clients and customers targeted by a company and current and future clients. Therefore, the business model canvas should accurately assess the desired market share. Data from feasibility studies should be utilized to evaluate the veracity of predictions and the feasibility of attaining the objectives indicated in the business model canvas. The total effect on market share should be taken into account, taking into account the added impact, the opportunity cost, and the risk that sales and market share will be taken away by other products, among other things.

What the general public thinks of this potentially profitable sector is difficult to say. Is it feasible to add value by making it available? What is the monetary value of this item? Is it possible that the company's mission, purpose, and essential principles may be compromised due to providing these clients? After completing all of the aforementioned assessments and identifying the ideal clients and customer groups, the next step is to develop a plan for gaining these new clients. To be successful, it is vital to judging the channels used to attract customers. Finally, it is possible to finish the purchase using one of the platforms indicated below:

- Internet marketing is a kind of marketing that takes place entirely on the internet rather than in person.
- Increasing your clientele base via recommendations or using current customers is a possibility.
- Advertisements printed on paper are referred to as "print advertisements."
- Radio advertising is a kind of public relations.
- It is a wonderful idea to provide free trials to customers.
- Use the internet to communicate with your consumers.

It is possible to reach out to customers in today's fast-paced and digitally altered world via several channels. To advertise your company's products, you must first establish your company's presence in the marketplace and make that presence noticed by customers. The advantages of information dissemination and the comfort of engaging with customers on a more personal level are all brought about by the digitalization of the globe. There are, however, certain disadvantages to using it. In this information-rich age, customers have greater access to information. They can better compare the company's products and other activities directed toward customer satisfaction with those of national, regional, and international competitors and their own.

To maintain and build customer relationships, businesses today must go above and beyond what was required of them a generation ago compared to their predecessors. As a result of globalization and technological improvements, competition has increased and diversified, but it has also been brought straight to the doorsteps of businesses themselves. As a result, a considerable increase in the number of online venues and social media platforms companies may use to sell their products and connect with customers worldwide has occurred in recent years. As a business owner, it may be possible to use these online tools to your advantage to get your name out there and make a good impression on your clients.

These are the platforms on which they will be implemented:

- Websites
- Twitter
- Facebook
- WhatsApp
- In the corporate sector, advertising platforms promote products and services.
- Blogs

If feasible, you should also make your website seem professional and, if all feasible, include a blog where customers may connect with you. Your website's aesthetic appeal, curiosity, and addictiveness are essential if you want to attract and retain visitors. The internet platform must advertise and sell its image, corporate reputation, brand name, and goods to consumers while also requesting information about them to become more familiar with the company.

Consider spending some time conversing with customers, asking questions to get insight into their ideas, and responding to their enquiries to lay the groundwork for future research. A more in-depth look into the customer's history, expectations, views, and perceptions of the company and its products allows for a more comprehensive picture to be gathered from their responses and feedback. This information is crucial in building meaningful customer interactions via the use of a strong online presence that is both visible and accessible. The activities of other customers might also lead to the discovery of new consumers.

7.2 Customer referrals or recommendations

In addition to being vital in developing a strong customer base, the way you connect with your customers has the potential to produce sales and, ultimately, revenue for your company. A key marketing method for attracting new customers to a company's goods or services is called "viral marketing." One of a company's most important channels for marketing and distribution of products is its most loyal and satisfied customers. They also serve as a source of value creation for the company and its various stakeholders, including creditors, suppliers, customers, shareholders, and capital providers, among others.

Customers who are delighted with the company's value propositions and its products may prove to be a simple and cost-free resource for promoting the business and its products to additional prospective customers in the future. It is infectious, and people tell their friends and family about the outstanding service or high-quality products that the company has supplied them with. Whether planned or inadvertent, Amplification advertising will ensure that the brand is advertised more conveniently and cost-effectively, whether the advertising is paid or unpaid. Clients have been made into "sales agents" who are not company employees via a deceptive indirect procedure. Consequently, it is critical to remember that customer satisfaction has a two-fold effect: it results in a loyal client who also functions as a brand ambassador. Because satisfied customers may be more willing to aid a company in marketing its products in a timely and efficient manner, the business model canvas should contain measurements that may be utilized to leverage a company's competitive advantage.

7.3 Method of maintaining customer relationships

It is not sufficient to just please a client to keep them as a customer. Customers now expect more from their business connections than simply a transactional transaction. Having a sense of accomplishment is not good enough. Perhaps a little more acknowledgement and a feeling of ownership over the things and a sense of being appreciated would be sufficient compensation. A company's success is dependent on its willingness to go the extra mile. Numerous tactics may aid firms in going above and beyond in their attempts to retain customers and build long-term relationships with them. Some examples of these strategies are mentioned below.

- Recognize and express gratitude to your customers.
- Feedback should be solicited and acted upon as appropriate.
- Demonstrate your gratitude and appreciation by saying "thank you."
- Always go the extra mile to make a difference in someone's life.

7.4 Increasing customers in your business

Customers may be obtained via several different means. The same tactics used to retain them can also be used to help them grow and develop. A few examples of what you may do are referrals, upsells, and cross-sells, to name a few. In addition, it is possible to apply a range of extra strategies to boost the number of clients. The following are some of the most significant: Understand the customer and the business for whom you are providing services. For a business to properly match the wants of consumers with the services or products supplied by the company, the business must get a deeper understanding of those demands (their objectives, ambitions, vision, purpose, expectations, and general preferences). The ability to have complete knowledge of its customers gives a company a competitive advantage over its rivals since its products "hit the bullseye" when it comes to meeting the expectations of its customers.

If a company's products are of excellent quality, it will swiftly establish itself as a favourite supplier. The company strives to personalize its things precisely in the way that customers want, which results in a more advantageous interaction for all parties concerned. The essential thing is to develop the best suitable solution for the given circumstance. It may be beneficial for businesses such as those in the garment sector to know their customers' age and fashion preferences since this information may help salespeople decide whom to alert when particular sorts of things become available in their stores. Since they have a long-standing relationship with the business, it is conceivable for a salesperson to set aside something, particularly for a specific customer. An increase in the number of customers is demonstrated in this case, and the consumer feels valued. Due to their greater awareness of their customers' needs, small businesses may profit from the advantages of being smaller.

As a result, they can deliver more tailored services to their customers. The fact that small businesses enjoy this competitive advantage over giant organizations is significant. Understanding your company well enough to respond to shifting consumer expectations is essential for success. Ensure you have an appropriate mix of resources and time to provide excellent service to your current clients while seeking new business. Please keep in mind that the increase in the customer base has a dual impact on the company. Small companies must strive to balance retaining current customers and enticing potential new ones to join the fold. Clients who have remained with the business for an extended period must be kept satisfied, and their morale increased for them to feel valued by the company, which always results in their spending more money.

Therefore, it is vital to seek out and foster new relationships until they reach a mature stage of development. To differentiate yourself from the competition, make sure you deliver efficient and unique customer service. When it comes to establishing a business, providing the best possible customer service is one of the most crucial factors. When customers feel calm and secure in their dealings with a company, they are more inclined to spend more time with that company. Consumers may be sceptical and cautious the first time they interact with a business, but as they acquire confidence that they are in great hands, they become more inclined to place their trust in the company and spend more money with them.

Maintaining a delicate balance in customer service requires that the business consistently evaluate its performance concerning the needs and expectations of customers and that corrective measures are implemented as soon as possible when value propositions are not delivered as promised or when customers are dissatisfied with a specific issue. If you get feedback in person or on social media platforms, you should consider using it as a starting point for taking corrective action. You should also utilize it to continuously enhance the operations of your business's operations and your relationship with customers.

Make use of the networks that are now accessible to you. Networks and linkages that already exist are collectively referred to as "social capital," and a company may use them to enhance sales and expand the number of customers it serves. Some businesses get new consumers due to their participation in networking events. For instance, a construction contractor may recommend another company within its network that provides plumbing services to be considered for a project where plumbing work is required to be done. By providing outstanding customer service and establishing trust among your network members, you will be able to extend your client base via networking. Another technique of receiving recommendations is via word-of-mouth referrals. Creating alliances with other businesses to bring customers together under one roof while also extending the consumer base may be a simple and efficient way to accomplish both goals. Again, it is taking advantage of social media platforms.

CHAPTER 7: IMPROVING CUSTOMER RELATIONSHIP

8

Chapter 8: Why Write a Business Plan

When you go back to your high school years, the memory of being assigned the task of writing a 30-page term paper for one of your courses comes rushing back to mind. It's safe to say that, if you're anything like most of your peers, the very thought of this assignment brought tears to your eyes almost instantly.

Let's fast forward to the current day and discuss that as an entrepreneur, you are either starting a business or seeking outside financing to assist in the development of your company. You are struck with dread as you realize that you will be expected to develop a business plan to advance your company's goals and objectives. Making a business plan is likely to bring up memories of your high school years when you were charged with writing research papers for your English class.

Don't be scared by this. Refrain from acting on your instinct to leave. Of course, I understand that developing a plan takes much time. However, it is definitely worth the time and effort to see the business planning process through to completion since it has so many valuable lessons to teach you about your business and the opportunity you are presented with.

Some people who run small businesses or start businesses have found out that there are many benefits to going through the business planning process through trial and error. To figure out how long your business can last and how well it can grow and succeed, you need to have a good look at the whole thing.

- Business plans are great tools for ensuring that the company's stakeholders want to achieve the same goals. They make people work together to solve any problems they might have in a single action plan.
- A business plan is a powerful tool for communicating your vision, purpose, values, and objectives to the stakeholders who will assist you in launching and growing your company—suppliers, partners, customers, employees, and members of your company's board of directors—clearly and understandably.
- Companies may benefit from having a complete understanding of the opportunities and challenges in their market and industry and the capacity to build strategies and tactics that directly respond to the needs of their customers and clients.
- Your company is indeed in a competitive environment, and the extent to which you can separate your company from the competitors will determine your level of success. Developing a business plan makes it possible to get valuable competitive information and establish how you will differentiate your products, services, and value proposition from the competition.
- According to Business Insider, understanding your company's business and its customers can help you develop the most successful team for your company. The management team didn't have the skills, ability, or experience to take advantage of what the industry offers. As a result, many companies with great products and big markets haven't made it or haven't reached their full potential.

Early and rising stages of growth: A well-thought-out business plan will show how the company will be set up and how it will work. It will also include a detailed strategy and a timetable. The ability to investigate "what-if" scenarios and establish contingency plans if your Plan A does not come out as expected- a situation that happens on an almost daily basis is very valuable.

Take joy in the planning process for your company's future. Spend some time drafting a business plan that you will be proud to put your name on so that you can demonstrate your commitment to your company. It is certainly worth the time and effort to go through the process.

8.1 Establish the authenticity of your company

It might be exciting to start a business from a hobby you've been doing for a long time, but this doesn't mean that the business will make money.

When developing a company plan, one of the first tasks is to conduct market research on your target audience and competitors. Learn all you can about market trends and what your competitors have done to succeed (or fail) in their respective ventures. It is possible that, after more examination, you may realize that the original thought you had is unlikely to be successful.

Although this may be frustrating, you can always modify your original plan to meet market needs better. Having a thorough understanding of your sector and your possible competitors and clientele can greatly increase your chances of success. By detecting early issues, you may build techniques to deal with them rather than deal with them as they arise. This saves you from having to deal with problems as they arise. Before investing a lot of time and money into your business, it is best to know whether or not it will be a success. This way, you can plan ahead of time.

8.2 Creating a foundation for the future success

Let us consider the following scenario: you wish to start a green cosmetics company. The statement "I'm starting a clean beauty company!" would not be enough because there are many different ways to go. Before proceeding, you must be crystal clear about the specific items you desire to make and why you wish to do so.

You will also use your first market research results to generate financial projections, goals, objectives, and an overview of the operational needs of your company's operations. Establishing this foundation ahead of time is critical because you will be making critical business decisions very early in the process, and failing to do so will jeopardize your chances of success.

You may go back to the goals you set for your company in your strategy to see how well you've done and which areas need more attention. Every aspect of your business plan demands a comprehensive assessment of your future business strategy before moving forward with your plans. A well-thought-out plan gives your business a strong foundation to build for future growth and progress. Early on in the development and launch of your new product, you will spend less time fixing things and more time focusing on your customers and making money, which will lead to more money.

8.3 Obtain funding and investment

Every new company needs capital to get off the ground and become profitable. However, having requested a loan does not mean that the bank will finance it. Instead, they will want to know what you're spending the money on, where it's going, and whether or not you will have the financial ability to repay it.

If you want investors to be a part of your financing plan, they may probably have issues with your company's pricing techniques and revenue patterns.

Here's how to address such worries. Additionally, investors can withdraw their investment if they think their money is not being used effectively. To judge your progress over time and establish whether or not you are meeting the goals you promised them, they will want something they can refer to. Finally, they are interested in learning whether or not their investment was profitable.

To get loans or communicate with investors, you should first complete the Financial Considerations section of your business plan, which will motivate you to estimate costs and set revenue objectives ahead of time. To avoid being unprepared for your meeting with investors, you would have already worked on and finished your plan.

8.4 Recruiting appropriate staff

You may find that, once you've completed your business plan and have a clear knowledge of your strategy, objectives, and financial needs, there are milestones you need to reach that necessitate the learning of skills that you don't currently have, such as marketing, to complete. In addition, you'll likely have to hire new staff to fill up the gaps created by the layoffs.

When you have a strategic plan to offer to prospective partners and employees, you can demonstrate that they are not signing on the dotted line for a ship that will sink. It is easier for them to understand why you want them to be on your team and why they should work with you on a project if the goals are clear and attainable.

8.5 Make your needs and desires known

It will be tough to explain the validity of your corporation to all of the people involved if they do not have a clear grasp of how your company will work. As a result of your business plan, you will have a complete grasp of how your company will run, which will make it easier for you to describe this to others.

Although you may have previously obtained financing from banks and entered into agreements with investors, the requirements of a business are always changing. For example, your company's growth will require acquiring extra financial resources, including new partners or extending your service and product offerings. By looking at how well your business plan is doing to meet your goals, you may be able to get more people on your team at different points in the process.

As a result, the process of selling your company becomes less complicated. Investing in a company that will go bankrupt quickly after signing the purchase agreement is not something a buyer will want to do. Instead, they are on the lookout for a lucrative, well-established company.

A business plan that includes milestones that you can demonstrate you have already completed may be used to explain to prospective buyers how you have achieved success in your field. In addition, you may be able to use your accomplishments to negotiate higher price points that are more in line with the value of your company's assets.

8.6 Have a business strategy in place

In conclusion, having a company plan can assist you in feeling more confident about your new venture. In addition, a grasp of what your company needs to thrive will be provided, and an outline of the methods used to achieve those goals. Some people have had a lifetime dream of turning their passions into lucrative business ventures, and a well-crafted business plan may be the key to helping them achieve their goals.

Fundamentally, having a company plan will help you make better decisions since it will guide you through the process. When it comes to making decisions and dealing with crises, entrepreneurship may seem like a never-ending activity. However, small businesses may not always have the luxury of having the time to sit down and think through all of the ramifications of a given action before moving forward. In this case, an excellent business plan might help you reach your goals. In developing a business plan, you will be able to foresee and forecast the results of some of the most crucial decisions your company will face in the future.

Creating a detailed business plan is a time-consuming task; you must set aside some time to sit down and consider important aspects of your corporation before getting started, such as your marketing strategy and the products or services you will provide. However, you can foresee and respond to many challenging questions before they arise. Furthermore, going further into your major techniques may help you better grasp how those options will affect your overall strategy, which is beneficial.

8.7 Ironing out the kinks

Before developing their company strategy, entrepreneurs must first ask themselves many challenging questions and take the required time to develop well-researched and analytical responses. While the paper itself may never be seen again, the process of making it will help you better communicate your ideas and find flaws in your approach.

8.8 Demonstrate the viability of the company

For many businesses, passion serves as the driving force behind their operations. However, even though emotions can be strong motivators, they aren't always a good way to show that something is true.

One of the most important steps between having a vision and having a great business is figuring out exactly how you're going to turn that vision into a reality. Financial projections might help you decide whether or not your brilliant idea makes good business sense.

8.9 Create detailed objectives and performance indicators

The lack of a company plan may lead to arbitrary objectives with no rhyme or reason to support their achievement. If you have a company plan, making such requirements more relevant and influential is feasible. They are also beneficial in that they can keep you accountable for your long-term vision and goals, and they can give insights into how your approach is (or isn't) coming together as time progresses.

8.10 Effectively communicate your objectives

If you're in charge of a team of 100 people or two people, there will be moments when you won't be able to be there to make every decision yourself. Assume that the business strategy serves as a replacement teacher who is accessible to answer questions anytime there is a gap in the course schedule. Explanation: Explain to your staff that if they ever have a question, they should consult the business plan to identify the best course of action to follow if they cannot get a satisfactory response from you.

When you share your company plan with team members, you can guarantee

START WITH A BUSINESS PLAN

that everyone knows what you're doing and why you're doing it. You can also ensure that everyone is on the same page regarding long-term objectives.

8.11 Comprehensive grasp of the larger terrain

No business is an island, and although you may have a good understanding of what is going on inside your walls, it is just as important to be aware of what is going on in the rest of the market. Developing a business plan can help you better understand your competitors and the market you compete with. It can also show you customer trends and preferences, possible disruptions, and other things that aren't always obvious when you write them down.

While it's true that starting your own company is a risky activity, the risk becomes far more manageable when put to the test against a well-written business plan. Knowledge of how to calculate revenue and expenditure predictions, the development of logistical and operational plans, and a grasp of the market and competitive environment may help reduce the risk factor associated with a job that is fundamentally insecure by nature. Making a plan for your business and making good decisions will help you leave less to chance and have the clearest picture of your company's future.

8.12 Things to take into consideration

Developing a business plan is the first step in establishing a new company from scratch. Even if you just want to start a small business, you must have a business plan before proceeding. Creating a business plan, in general, involves detailing the course of your company's activities. It will include information about your company that has been written from your point of view, among other things.

According to most people, these plans are meaningless since there is no need for them to write down information that they already know in their thoughts. Instead, consider the following ideas to understand better why a business strategy is crucial.

First and foremost, developing a company strategy can only be accomplished after conducting a comprehensive study of the existing circumstances. Because of this, you will be able to define your company's goals and devote your whole focus to achieving them.

You may be able to use your company's aims to attract new clients. For example, examine the following scenario: A client only picks an outsourced service provider if it is established that the provider can do the task correctly and effectively. In these cases, your company's strategies will be able to show how effective your services are to people who might buy them.

When establishing a business plan, you may discover previously unnoticed weaknesses in your company's operations. One of the most important benefits of having a plan in place is that you can see problems before they happen, which can save a lot of money and reputation in the long run.

If you don't plan your company, you'll surely follow your own rules and lose out on valuable opportunities. For example, consider the following scenario: if you were tasked with developing a company's strategy, you would seek feedback from other experts who had appropriate experience and knowledge. The result will be that you will be able to get insight into what you should avoid in your business.

9

Chapter 9: Avoiding Mistakes When Writing a Business Plan

W hen you are ready to establish a new business venture, a business plan guide is ideal for beginning your research and planning. However, unless you've already invested in a book on writing business plans or are using a template to guide you through the process, it's likely that these resources will only cover the steps necessary to complete your written report and will fail to point out the critical mistakes that the vast majority of first-time business owners make. So, let's put the step-by-step guidance aside for the time being and focus on the errors you should avoid making in the real world.

9.1 Do not put it off any longer!

Developing a company plan may be a time-consuming and complex undertaking: The ability to put things off may come naturally to you while you are focused on the more interesting areas of your company's operations. For example, new business owners sometimes put off their scheduled meeting with the bank until the day before and then scurry to create a business plan every evening. You probably have a good idea of what occurred.

Avoid delaying choosing till you have more time on your hands: There is no such thing as a second chance. Instead, make your planning a top priority for the next week by clearing your calendar for the whole week. If this is not an option, or if it is not practical, schedule a certain amount of time each day to devote only to preparing specified activities. You may have heard the saying, "If you fail to plan, plan to fail," which means "If you don't prepare, you're planning to fail."

9.2 Do not confuse profit with cash flow

It is quite likely that, unless you have a history in accounting, you will evaluate your company's performance in terms of profits earned. Profit may be calculated easily by dividing sales by expenses, which results in a profit. However, profits are not always translated into cash for businesses.

Your profit estimate does not consider, among other things, the amount of cash you have locked up in production expenditures for goods that have not yet been sold or the amount of money due to you by customers for sales that have already been made. Although your company seems to be "profitable," it is possible that your bank account is overdrawn.

Check to make sure that your written plan includes a cash flow table, which will help to guarantee that everything goes smoothly. To be precise, you should give the monthly cash flow for the company's first two years and the annual cash flow for the remainder of the company's existence.

Avoid being emotionally attached to your thoughts. Too many business plans spend pages and pages describing the "newness" and "uniqueness" of the idea they are presenting rather than focusing on the concept itself. Realistically, it is more common for investors to want to invest in people than in ideas.

This is because individuals are the only ones capable of implementing the processes necessary to bring the notion to reality.

If you want to get your reader's attention, instead of waxing lyrical about your company's concept, draw their attention to the precise ways you propose to put this amazing business idea into reality.

9.3 Overcoming your feelings of fear

It is possible that if you have never written a business plan before, the endeavour would seem as overwhelming as conquering Mount Everest. On the other hand, developing a plan is not nearly as tough as you thought, as with most new challenges. You are not writing a doctoral dissertation or the next great novel?

What are you working on? You should make use of any business plan guide that you have purchased. You will be able to discover valuable items such as books, software programs, and template papers in a short period. Take note that you must chew and bite your way through an elephant, so sink your teeth into it and chew some more.

9.4 Do not go crazy on marketing

If possible, avoid employing business jargon that is vague and meaningless, such as phrases like "best," "highest quality," and "unsurpassed customer service." Your reader will lose interest and respect if you utilize hyperbole that is not supported by quantitative evidence. Recall that the purpose of a plan is to accomplish particular objectives, which demands monitoring and follow-up tools and techniques. Maintain focus on specific dates, management responsibilities, budgets, and verifiable milestones to guarantee that your goals are fulfilled on time. Instead of using more words, consider using fewer words and more numbers instead.

9.5 Do not shoehorn everyone into a single category

Business plans may be used for several purposes: They should be written so that they represent the specific reason for which they are being utilized. For example, your strategy might be used to start a business or just improve the efficiency of your present operation. For example, it's feasible that your objective is to advertise the notion of a whole new company to a single potential business partner.

Following your objectives: Your business plan may be intended to get a small company loan, or it may be necessary to secure millions of dollars in venture capital funding. For each of these reasons, the information necessary would be different, and it would need to be presented in a different way to meet the needs of a varied range of readers. However, if you have a clear mental picture of your target reader in mind at all times, your business plan will stay on track.

9.6 Take time to reflect

Positivity is a fantastic benefit in almost any situation: It would be impossible for a business owner to produce the necessary energy to launch a new venture if they did not already have it. The present, however, is not the appropriate moment to make bold predictions about the future. You must be prepared to show that your company's growth chart is based on an "industry average" of fifteen per cent annual growth. Provide proof to back up your claims, and if in doubt, be less optimistic in your remarks.

Don't wait any longer to start developing your approach: Don't wait until you have enough time, don't wait until you have the right staff. Most importantly, don't wait until you have an urgent situation that necessitates the development of a strategy before beginning to work on it. As an alternative, simply go ahead and do it. Recognize that you need a business plan and that your first step should be to put together a draft of your original company strategy to get things started. Get the first draft up and running as soon as possible, and keep upgrading it to keep it current with your company's requirements and objectives. Although likely, your plan may never be finished, the important thing to remember is that you are still making preparations. You should be thinking about ways to make your business better all of the time.

Keep in mind that cash and earnings are not the same things: Between the two, there is a major difference in approach. It is possible that waiting for customers to pay you will have a debilitating effect on your financial situation, even though it has no impact on your profits. For example, inventory loading is time-consuming and adds little value to your business's profitability. However, cash flow is much more important than profits since profits are an accounting word and money in the bank—profits are not utilized to pay your debts and so have no impact on profits.

Don't allow your priorities to get muddled: Having a strategy that is concentrated on three or four key objectives is a strategy that is both concentrated and strong. The vast majority of individuals can distinguish between three or four primary themes. It is not possible to have real priorities in a plan that has 20 priority items in it.

Don't put too much focus on the company's overall business idea: According to the entrepreneur, it is not the concept itself that adds value to a company, but rather the business that has already been developed on top of it that adds value to the notion. When employees arrive at work every morning, phone calls are answered, things are made, bought, and delivered, services are provided, and customers pay their bills, a business idea becomes a profitable business. Either you develop a business plan that outlines how you intend to build a company around that wonderful idea, or you give up and give up the ghost. A great company is not formed just based on a fantastic idea.

Don't confuse having a strategy with actually carrying out the plan: You must have both to be successful. And you're planning process does not come to an end after your strategy is completed. The value of a plan is found in the implementation it generates, and implementation starts the day you and your team come to terms with the key components of your plan's content. Take into consideration that your business plan is never finished—you are always updating it or should be since reality is always speeding ahead. You'll never be able to distinguish between a plan and reality unless you have a plan that establishes markers. So make your strategy a reality rather than merely writing it down.

During the first 12 months, don't change the information: I'm referring to your financials, milestones, dates, responsibilities, and deadlines, among other things. In addition to having plenty of information on hand when it comes to assigning tasks to individuals, defining activity dates, and stating what is expected to occur as well as who will be required to bring it about, you must also have plenty of information on hand when it comes to planning for the future. These details are quite important. A company's strategy is pointless if it is not implemented.

Don't get too caught up in the details until later in life: The focus here is on planning rather than accounting, and you're merely making predictions in a system full of uncertainty. As important as monthly details are initially, they quickly become a waste of time and effort as the year progresses. In light of the uncertainty surrounding your sales projection, how can you predict your monthly cash flow for three years into the future? Sure, in the great conceptual literature, you can plan in five, ten or even twenty-year, respectively, but you can't plan in monthly detail beyond the first year unless you start from scratch. After that, nobody anticipates it, and no one believes it to be true.

Making projections: Don't make unreasonably optimistic "hockey stick" projections about your company's revenues increasing dramatically soon. While it is true that this happens around once per generation, no one believes it in a business plan since everyone says it. No investor will tell you that even though your sales have been flat up to this point, they believe that your sales will soar to dizzying heights after they have invested their money. Unless you've genuinely built a once-in-a-generation company whose sales will take off, you should include as much bottom-up information into your prediction as possible so that even the most jaded investor will believe it.

Don't write too much at one time: Maintain conciseness in your company plan and concentrate on your primary objectives. It is not a doctoral thesis; rather, it is a commercial plan. Keep your thoughts focused on the main issues, and use bullet points to keep the most critical aspects concentrated and brief.

Formatting: Don't be concerned with the technicalities of the formatting. There has never been a time when a corporate plan failed because the page headers were not colour coded. Don't overcomplicate your plan by using several fonts, multiple colours, or complicated page layouts. On the other hand, don't try to hide the most important information. Keep things simple, and don't get too worked up over the tiny details.

10

Chapter 10: Quick Tips for Writing a Business Plan

T he drafting of a business plan may be particularly advantageous during the early phases of a company's growth, providing a guiding force in the uncertainties inherent in starting a company, such as distractions and, at times, rapid changes. If you work for a big company, you should think of your business plan as a living, breathing document that helps you make decisions and grow your company, not just a record.

- Has the skill of developing a business plan become second nature to you? It is unnecessary to be worried about those who have not completed the procedure since it is not complex. It shouldn't be difficult to write a well-structured company plan if you follow some useful guidelines in this area.
- Because a business plan is an effective sales tool, it must be written attractively and understandably so that there is no uncertainty in the minds of prospective investors when they read it.
- This implies that the language used must be plain, uncomplicated, and easy to comprehend. Put forth an effort to focus primarily on the most important themes and avoid being sidetracked by unimportant details.

It is crucial to identify what should be eliminated and included in the analysis. To make sure that all of the important parts are covered, write down a list.

- Set fair, consistent, and clear goals for your company and goals that are likely to be attainable given the way your company works.
- Among the issues to discuss should be your target customers, the operation of the intended market, and how you propose to fulfil the needs and wishes of your target audience.
- Give examples of how you know your sponsor's interests and needs very well.
- You should avoid over-expressing your excitement about your products or disclosing details about your production procedures to outside parties unless you have their permission beforehand.
- Demonstrate that your team has a diverse range of abilities and a proven track record of accomplishment to capitalize on market opportunities in a way that creates profit for the company. Furthermore, show the committee that your team is committed to the idea for the long run.
- Whenever possible, it is ideal if you address issues and risks while also describing how to cope with them in particular circumstances. In addition, ensure that your company's strategy is complete, easily accessible, and does not need the inclusion of additional information or explanation.
- In your business plan, you will find these basic rules. They will help you build a strategy that meets your business's goals and will be a good resource in the future.

10.1 Demonstrate your concern

Allow your passion for your company to shine through; convey to employees and investors why you are committed to the company (and why they should too). Provide a comprehensive list of appendices, which may contain team members' curriculum vitae, customer personas that have been built, product demonstrations, and examples of internal and external communications.

10.2 A reference point

Each piece of information you provide about the market, your competitors, and your customers should be backed up by reputable and relevant data and sources. Research for your business plan should take you far longer to complete than the actual authoring of the document. Therefore, consider keeping track of your research to supply supporting documentation to your stakeholders.

Demonstrate how you are different from the competition by exhibiting your points of differentiation. With every opportunity comes the possibility to underline how your product or service separates you from the competition and supports your target audience in addressing an issue they may be facing. Don't be afraid to bring up these distinguishing characteristics several times throughout the method.

10.3 Maintain your neutrality

As much as it is important to draw attention to your company and the benefits you provide your customers, it is also important to be impartial in the facts and research to back up your assertions. It's important to emphasize both the positive and negative aspects of your market research and financials; you want your shareholders to know that you've considered every potential scenario.

10.4 Understand what you want to achieve

It is vital that you understand the purpose of your plan before you begin studying and developing it. Make it clear whether you're developing your plan to get money, align teams, or provide direction to the company.

10.5 Determine your target audience

To be effective, your company's strategy must have a clearly defined aim, just as you must have a clearly defined audience. Who is it that you are addressing your letter to? Is there any fresh money coming in? Do you have any current workers on your payroll? Is there anybody who may be interested in collaborating?

10.6 Keep the use of jargon to a bare minimum

Make every effort to avoid using industry-specific jargon until required. Make your business plan easy to understand for all of your potential stakeholders. Jargon should be avoided at all costs; clear, concise language should be utilized. In part, this is because business plans are too long. As a result, they are less likely to be used as intended and are more likely to be forgotten or ignored by the people who work with them.

10.7 Do not be afraid to make updates

Business plans should develop in unison with the expansion of your company, which indicates that the document containing your business plan should also alter over time. Therefore, take the time to review and update your company's strategy as needed, and remember that having a plan in place is the most important thing, no matter how things change in the future.

Making a business plan shouldn't just be something to cross off your to-do list; it should be referred to and used in the way it was designed. Continue to keep your company's strategic plan close at hand and use it to influence decisions and lead your team in the years ahead of you.

Developing a business plan is a key first step when extending your company's operations. If you are just starting or have a well-established company, establishing a strong business plan is essential since it may serve as a key predictor of future success. It can serve as a solid foundation to build your future and flourish. It may serve as a frequent reminder to employees and consumers about what your business stands for and the direction in which you're heading the right way, which is beneficial. As an alternative, it might show investors that your company, its employees, and its purpose are worthwhile their time and money to pursue.

Any company's success is dependent on its ability to establish a goal that it wishes to attain. Your business needs to set and meet these goals to succeed in the long run. Preparing a business plan is essential if you want to clearly explain the aspects of your company on which you want to focus your efforts. Business cases may guide you through the ordinary course of your company's operations. However, they can also supply you with vital information when problems develop. To write an effective business case, you must first develop a written summary of your objectives, followed by a detailed plan of action that will be employed to attain those objectives after they have been determined. Here are

10.7.1 Suggestions for developing an effective business plan

Set objectives that are within your grasp and reachable

Develop a business case to establish your company's goals and objectives as the starting point. When starting a business planning process, it is vital to clearly define the goals and objectives that you want your company to attain as soon as possible. If you have a realistic perspective when creating these objectives, it will be easier to attain results within your business's reach.

Conservatism is something that should be practised

Developing a timetable and spending chart for the costs you will incur due to carrying out your company's strategic objectives is critical. Although entrepreneurs must retain a minimalist approach, it is also important to refrain from devoting excessive attention to financial requirements or schedules. It is also critical not to be too hopeful while establishing a business since several things may go wrong during the first stages. This is true for enterprises since capital requirements, deadlines, sales, and profitability are all hard to foresee with any degree of precision. This is especially true for startups.

Construct a simply understandable business plan.

The use of simple language will be advantageous to you in constructing your outline, so make use of it. On the other hand, avoid using technical phrases that will seem out of place in your company's strategic business strategy. It will just make it more difficult to comprehend your difficulties.

Make a plan for dealing with hardship.

The ability to foresee and prepare for any hurdles your company may encounter is crucial when building your business plans and strategies. In the early phases of your company's development, you will notice that there are certain challenges that you will encounter as you go through the normal course of business operations. These difficulties will be discussed more below. Don't ignore or dismiss your problems; instead, come up with a plan for dealing with them if they happen again.

Make a concentrated effort to achieve your short-term aims

This is not to say that you should not plan ahead of time if you want to be successful in the long run. The importance of focusing on short-term goals

94

cannot be overstated, however. Concentrate on milestones that are more readily reached, and make revisions to your plans as you advance through the company to prepare for long-term projections and forecasts. At the current moment, it is more important for future projections to be consistent with your short-term achievements than they are otherwise.

Instead of emphasizing creativity, economics should be given precedence

Your company needs to be creative to differentiate itself from the competition. Even if your company is wonderful or uncommon, success may be difficult to achieve without careful consideration of money and a well-planned business strategy to get things off to a successful start.

Writing a business plan is not a straightforward task to do

As part of putting their original ideas into reality, an entrepreneur must first design the ideal blueprint for the company, which acts as a starting point for developing a great blueprint for the business. Non-profit business plans are useful for presenting to potential investors, but they can also serve as a guide to help you achieve your goals and objectives. At the same time, you go about your daily business. Therefore, it is up to you to learn some useful ideas to help you work on your company strategy.

Make your plan more manageable by breaking it down into sections

A business plan should be very well structured and easy to grasp, especially for those unfamiliar with your company's nature. This is especially true for those unfamiliar with your organisation's nature (e.g., investors, angel investors, venture capitalists).

Consult with someone who can provide a second opinion

Having another pair of eyes review your business plan is crucial once you have completed the first draft of the company plan. This is not just to discover and correct any mistakes but also to get feedback on other routes you may not have been aware of. What matters is that as many people as possible have a look at what you have. This can come in handy when you're looking for the last piece of the puzzle to complete the image you've created.

Prepare to make revisions to your work

Every company's strategy is subjected to several iterations. The odds of doing it right on the first try are slim to none, and even if you do, there is a significant probability that it was done incorrectly in the first place. Therefore, it's important to gather feedback once you've presented your company plan to others. After all, after you've launched a product, your approach may need to be altered in response to the demands of customers and consumers. Additionally, be sure to update your strategy at least once every few months to be certain that when it comes time to meet with investors, they will be looking at the most up-to-date version of your plan.

Consider yourself a business owner

Keep in mind that you are always in the position of the investor. Always remember to stress the potential profitability of your business while also recognizing that you will be competing against other businesses in the market. These are the top two criteria that investors will be looking for when making investment choices soon. Make a concerted attempt to combine both components into your executive summary so that investors can see what you've accomplished immediately. Investors may also be interested in additional characteristics such as industry-leading gross profit margins, intellectual property rights, brand expansion opportunities, customer con-tracts, recurring revenue potential, and strategic relationships with larger companies, among other things.

Recognize and understand your target market

Before starting any company endeavour, it is vital to understand your target market thoroughly. You must be aware of the supplies you will need to complete the building project on time and within budget. Keeping track of other companies involved in the same sector as yours is essential for business success. Distinguish yourself from them by explaining how you will be able to complete tasks more quickly and effectively as a result of your newfound knowledge of a full explanation of how and where you want to sell your items, as well as the amount of money it would cost you, is essential to draw clients to your location. According to industry standards, a client's value should be three or more times the cost of procuring a client.

Check to ensure that your profit margin calculations are accurate

Profit margins should be reported as a percentage of total revenue rather than a fixed percentage of total revenue. In most cases, the profit margin is computed as net income divided by revenue or as net profit divided by sales, depending on the context of the calculation. It quantifies the amount of money a company earns; that is, every dollar generated via sales is considered in this calculation. These margins are very helpful when comparing your company to a competitor's. For example, a higher profit margin would imply that the business is more profitable and that the company's expenses are better managed than they were in the previous period. Take care to compare averages with those of other companies in the same industry. Determine if your company's performance is at the high or low end of the range when compared to the performance of the rest of the market.

Recognize the potential threats

In writing, you and your colleagues should meticulously document operational risks that your company may face in the future. When it comes to gaining investors' trust, you must be open to new ideas and be prepared to alter your business practices. These investors like it when you are open to new ideas, and as a consequence, you and your investor will establish a stronger bond as a result of your willingness to be open to new ideas. We propose that you compile a list of the most serious risks that might affect your sales to mitigate them. During this period, you must be willing to learn about and appreciate a broad range of different options. You must be open to new experiences if you want to succeed.

Make your forecasts as detailed as possible while you're making them

Business plans should not be produced just to be comprehendible by you and your colleagues. The information in your excel sheet will be understandable to you, without a doubt, but other potential investors will not have the time or interest to figure out what your sheet is saying to them. So take care to clarify your points clearly and thoroughly and provide introductions and descriptions that will aid the reader in comprehending your findings and conclusions.

Give a detailed explanation of how the money will be utilized
There should be a statement of how the money is expected to be spent in any business strategy. Maintain transparency by distributing the revenues to the proper resources and equitable amounts. To avoid prospective investors' believing that investing in your project is the equivalent of burning or throwing their money away, it is critical that you pay close attention to this section. It is common for income to be spent on product development, intellectual property filings, equipment acquisition, loan repayment, and marketing activities rather than on any other purpose.

Establish a precise timetable with specified goals for each task
This section of the business plan is likely to be one of the most important sections of the entire plan. Try to be completely honest with yourself: is this something you believe you can accomplish? Your company's success depends on the commitment of investors to carefully monitor the achievement of these milestones throughout the entire process. If investors choose to participate in one company, you must ensure that they are dedicated to closely observing the accomplishment of these benchmarks throughout the entire process.

The inability to contact them may cause serious problems
If at all possible, try to incorporate management milestones into your strategy. Separate your project milestones from your product milestones and make sure that both parts are clear and understandable to everyone involved.

11

Chapter 11 - Conclusion

A business plan is a strategy that gets you from where you are today to where you want to be in the future, so don't forget to have one! We have highlighted the main points to consider when writing one for your business. It's not easy to put a plan together, especially when you're just beginning. Here I have compiled a step-by-step guide to help you write a simple and successful business plan that will draw attention and give you a leg up in the market.

We hope you enjoyed our book about writing a business plan. This is a great place to start for anyone trying to learn how to write a business plan. We know that not every business plan will be successful, but with the information provided in this book, I hope that you will be able to create a plan that has a good chance of succeeding.

12

Reference

- The Entrepreneur Small Business Encyclopedia has a section on "Business Plan." Entrepreneur. Obtain these details on October 29th, 2018. A business strategy may be defined as follows: A mission statement is a written document that explains a company's purpose, aims, and objectives. It also outlines its sales and marketing strategy and its financial status.
- Advice from Industry Veterans on How to Put Together a Workable Business Plan the United States of America is home to the prestigious Harvard Business School.
- This song first gained widespread attention because of Maran Jian and Selena. The following is a lesson about investing from "South Park." The epitome of idiocy, brought to you by the folks at the Motley Fool. A copy of the document in its original form.
- Services of advice and counsel provided by M&M, this page is preserved in the back machine's archive. You may have a good idea of where I'm going with this - "investors, banks, private equity firms, and other potential sources of finance are discussed. Those from whom you are attempting to solicit financial support. If this is the case, the strength of your business plan and the way you present it might be the deciding

factors in whether or not you are successful. If it is not convincing, the results for your company will not be as good." As a direct result of this, you won't have the ability to acquire an investment.

- "Business Plan Template," published by the United States Small Business Administration.
- In the context of a group assignment, students from the Carroll School of Management at Boston College collaborated on the creation of a business plan. Students are instructed by the business school to "take a comprehensive picture of the organisation and incorporate management-practice skills from every first-semester course" to generate a credible business plan. As a result, students in business programmes are increasingly allowed to put what they've learned in their classes into practice via business plan projects, which are becoming more common in business schools.
- Both Monica Dickon and Alistair R. Anderson contributed to this work (1 March 2011). Ambiguity and ambiguity are hallmarks of social entrepreneurship, as are competing narratives about the principles that should guide efforts to harmonies purpose and practice. An International Journal of Entrepreneurship and Management is What You'll Find Inside This Publication.

Printed in Great Britain
by Amazon

83616173R00068